The Financial Statements Playbook:

A Beginner's Guide to Reading, Understanding and Analysing Company Reports like Warren Buffett

Published by: John Messina

The Financial Statements Playbook

Copyright © 2024. All rights reserved.

You're welcome to enjoy this book, but please don't copy, share, or reproduce any part of it—whether by printing, scanning or any other method—without getting permission first from the author and publisher.

Disclaimer: This book, The Financial Statements Playbook, is designed to be an educational resource to help you understand financial analysis and investing. While every effort has been made to ensure the information is accurate and useful, please remember that financial concepts can be interpreted in different ways and the data may not reflect the latest developments. Always double-check the facts and consult a qualified financial advisor before making any investment or financial decisions.

The strategies, methods and ideas shared here are meant to give you a general understanding, not a one-size-fits-all solution. The author and publisher are not responsible for any losses or damages that may result from applying the information in this book.

Finally, this Book was created with the help of artificial intelligence (AI) to organise all the content and it was carefully reviewed to make it clear and beginner-friendly.

The Financial Statements Playbook

Contents

PREFACE: INTRODUCTION TO FINANCIAL STATEMENTS — 4

CHAPTER 1: UNDERSTANDING THE INCOME STATEMENT — 10

CHAPTER 2: DEMYSTIFYING THE BALANCE SHEET — 32

CHAPTER 3: CRACKING THE CASH FLOW STATEMENT — 54

CHAPTER 4: WARREN BUFFETT'S KEY RATIOS AND METRICS — 83

CHAPTER 5: FINANCIAL MANIPULATION AND RED FLAGS — 113

CONCLUSION: BRINGING IT ALL TOGETHER — 134

The Financial Statements Playbook

Preface: Introduction to Financial Statements

When I first started my journey into investing, the world of financial statements seemed like a daunting maze. The jargon, the numbers, the different types of reports—it all felt a bit overwhelming. But I soon realised that financial statements are the backbone of successful investing and understanding them was the key to making informed, sound decisions. Without a solid grasp of how to read and interpret these documents, you're left guessing, taking unnecessary risks and potentially missing out on great opportunities.

In this book, I want to show you just how powerful financial statements can be when used the right way. We'll break things down step by step so that, by the end, you'll not only understand what these documents are telling you but also how to use them to make smarter investment decisions.

As a value investor, much like Warren Buffett, I've come to rely heavily on financial statements to evaluate businesses. Buffett, often regarded as one of the greatest investors of all time, has always emphasised that the secret to successful investing is understanding the fundamentals of a business. He doesn't focus on short-term market trends or speculation. Instead, he looks at the financial health of a company—its ability to generate profits, manage debt and create consistent cash flow. Buffett believes that by understanding a company's financial reports, an investor can determine whether the company is truly undervalued, offering a good opportunity for long-term growth.

Why are financial statements so crucial for investors like Buffett? The answer lies in their ability to provide a clear picture of a company's past performance, current position and future potential. Without these reports, it would be nearly impossible to assess the financial strength of a company, let alone its true value. This is where a well-rounded understanding of financial statements becomes essential to any investor's toolkit.

Take, for example, the income statement. This document reveals how much money a company is earning and spending over a specific period. At first glance, it might seem like just a bunch of numbers, but once you know how to interpret them, you'll quickly see that the income statement offers vital insights into a company's profitability, efficiency and financial health. Investors like Buffett will look at things like revenue, gross profit and operating profit to assess how well the company is doing and whether it's managing its expenses wisely.

Another critical document is the balance sheet, which shows a company's financial position at a specific point in time. It lists everything the company owns (its assets), what it owes (its liabilities) and what's left over for shareholders (its equity). The balance sheet is particularly important for understanding a company's financial stability. Is it carrying too much debt? Does it have enough cash to cover short-term obligations? By carefully examining the balance sheet, investors can spot red flags, such as excessive debt, which could indicate financial trouble down the line.

Then, there's the cash flow statement, which tracks the flow of money into and out of the company. Cash flow is often considered one of the most important aspects of a company's financial health because it shows whether the business is generating enough cash to support its operations and invest in growth. Without solid cash flow, even a profitable company can struggle to stay afloat. Buffett often says that cash flow is one of the most telling signs of a company's true value.

As a beginner investor, it's easy to feel overwhelmed when looking at financial statements for the first time. But I want to reassure you that you don't need to be an accountant or financial expert to understand these documents. With a little time, patience and practice, you'll be able to read these reports and start drawing meaningful conclusions about a company's financial health.

When I first began, I didn't have all the answers. In fact, I made plenty of mistakes along the way. But over time, I learned how to read between the lines of financial reports and use that information to make smarter, more confident investment decisions. And now, I want to pass that knowledge on to you. This book is designed to give you a hands-on, practical approach to mastering financial statements. Each chapter will break down the key concepts in a straightforward way, using real-world examples that show you how to apply the information you learn to actual companies. You won't just be reading theory—you'll be practising how to evaluate real financial statements, just like a seasoned investor would.

Throughout the book, we'll look at the three main financial statements: the income statement, the balance sheet and the cash flow statement. Each of these documents plays a critical role in assessing the financial health of a business, and by the end of the book, you'll have the tools you need to evaluate any company, big or small.

For instance, in Chapter 1, we'll take a deep dive into the income statement. We'll break down the components, starting with revenue, the top line of the income statement, and move through to net income, the bottom line. You'll learn how to assess profit margins and spot potential concerns, like rising costs or shrinking margins. We'll also use real examples from well-known companies to show you how to interpret the data and understand what the numbers really mean.

In Chapter 2, we'll explore the balance sheet, a crucial tool for assessing a company's financial position. We'll explain how to read and understand assets, liabilities, and equity. By the end of this chapter, you'll know how to assess whether a company is financially stable, whether it has too much debt, and whether its assets are truly valuable. Again, we'll use real-world examples, including companies from the Australian market, to make these concepts relatable and practical.

Finally, in Chapter 3, we'll tackle the cash flow statement. You'll learn how to read the statement's three sections—operating, investing and financing activities—and understand the importance of cash flow for the long-term health of a business. We'll explore what makes strong cash flow and how to spot potential problems, like negative cash flow or declining cash reserves. Real examples will help you apply what you learn to actual businesses.

But it doesn't stop there. After you've learned how to read and understand these documents, I'll show you how to put it all together. In the final chapters, we'll focus on practical applications and case studies. You'll be able to look at a company's financial reports and assess whether it's worth investing in, just like a seasoned professional. We'll also talk about how to spot red flags and potential issues, helping you avoid the costly mistakes that many beginners make when they don't fully understand the financials.

By the end of this book, you won't just be able to read financial statements—you'll be able to analyse them, make informed decisions and confidently evaluate any company you're interested in. And most importantly, you'll be able to use this knowledge to make smarter, more successful investment decisions.

Remember, investing is a journey and mastering financial statements is one of the most important steps on that path. It may feel overwhelming at first, but with the right guidance and a little practice, you'll quickly gain the confidence you need to make informed, educated decisions. Take it one step at a time and soon you'll be analysing financial reports like a pro.

Happy reading and investing!

John Messina

Chapter 1: Understanding the Income Statement

What is the Income Statement?

When you hear the term "income statement," you might picture a complicated list of numbers with little to no context, but nothing could be further from the truth. The income statement, also known as the profit and loss statement, is one of the most important tools in understanding a company's financial performance. In the simplest terms, it shows you how much money a company is making—or losing—over a specific period, typically a quarter or a year.

Think of it as a snapshot of a company's profitability during a given period. It's the first place an investor should look when evaluating a business because it answers the fundamental question: is this company making money? And if so, how well is it managing its expenses to generate those profits?

For example, when Warren Buffett looks at a company, he wants to know two things upfront: Is the business consistently making a profit? And is it doing so efficiently? The income statement gives you the answers to these questions. It helps you assess the company's revenue, the costs associated with generating that revenue and ultimately the profits that are left over. The information you find here is crucial for understanding whether a company is thriving or just getting by.

Defining the Income Statement

So, what exactly does an income statement show? Essentially, it breaks down a company's revenues and expenses over a set period of time to give you a clear picture of its profitability. It's like a report card for a business's financial performance. If you were to compare it to running a household, the income statement would be similar to tracking your income versus your expenses for the month.

Here's the beauty of the income statement: it doesn't just show you how much a company made and spent. It's structured to highlight the company's ability to generate profits and manage costs, both of which are essential in evaluating the company's future growth prospects.

The income statement is made up of several key components, but it always follows the same general format. It starts with **revenue**, also known as sales or turnover and then subtracts various costs, including **Cost of Goods Sold**

(COGS) and **operating expenses**. The result is the **gross profit**, followed by **operating profit** and eventually, **net profit** at the bottom. Each of these numbers tells you something different about the company's operations and it's important to look at all of them in order to get a complete picture of how well a company is performing.

Why is this important? Well, for one thing, it helps you spot trends. Are revenues increasing over time? Are expenses growing at a faster rate than revenue? And most importantly, is the company able to generate consistent profits, or is it only profitable in certain months or quarters? By analysing the income statement, you can get a better idea of the company's ability to stay profitable over the long term, which is a key factor in making sound investment decisions.

Key Components of an Income Statement

Let's take a closer look at the key components of an income statement, so you can start to understand how they fit together. The structure of an income statement might seem a little complex at first, but with some practice, you'll start to recognise how each section plays a role in showing a company's financial health.

First, you'll notice **revenue** at the top. This is the total amount of money that the company has earned from selling goods or services during the period being reported. Revenue is a crucial starting point because it's the foundation of everything that follows. Without revenue, there's no business and without growth in revenue, a company can't scale. The key to evaluating revenue is looking at whether it's growing consistently over time. If revenue is stagnating or declining, that could be a red flag for future growth prospects.

Next, you'll see **Cost of Goods Sold (COGS)**, which refers to the direct costs associated with producing the goods or services that the company sells. For a retail company, this might include the cost of inventory, shipping and packaging. For a software company, it could include development costs or hosting fees. COGS is important because it tells you how much it costs the company to make its product or provide its service. Subtracting COGS from revenue gives you **gross profit**, which tells you how much money the company made after covering the direct costs of production.

After gross profit, you'll find **operating expenses**, which are the costs required to run the business but are not directly tied to the production of the goods or services. These include marketing, sales, administrative costs and other general overheads. Operating expenses are important to keep an eye on because they show you how efficiently a company is managing its day-to-day operations. If operating expenses are growing faster than revenue, it could indicate that the company is not controlling its costs effectively, which can erode profitability over time.

The next figure is **operating profit**, which is calculated by subtracting operating expenses from gross profit. Operating profit, sometimes called **earnings before interest and tax (EBIT)**, is a good indicator of how well the company is managing its core operations. This is the money that the company makes from running its business, before factoring in interest expenses or taxes.

Finally, we reach **net profit**, the bottom line of the income statement. This is the amount of money the company has left after subtracting all expenses, including interest and taxes. Net profit tells you how much profit the company is actually making, which is what matters most to investors. A business may be generating great revenue, but if its expenses are too high, it might not be making any real profit. Therefore, net profit is often considered the most important figure on the income statement.

To summarise: revenue tells you how much money the company is making, COGS and operating expenses show how much it costs to run the business, and gross profit, operating profit, and net profit tell you how well the company is managing its costs to generate a profit.

Real-life Example: Apple's Income Statement

Let's bring these concepts to life with a real-world example. Apple's income statement offers a perfect illustration of how all these components work together. We'll take a look at Apple's most recent financial report and break it down step by step to understand how these key components fit together.

In Apple's most recent income statement, we first see their **revenue**. For the 2023 fiscal year, Apple reported revenue of approximately $394 billion. That's a massive figure, but what's really interesting is how the revenue breaks down across different product categories—iPhones, Macs, iPads and services. By looking at this, we can start to understand where the company is making its money and whether those revenue streams are growing or shrinking. For instance, Apple's iPhone revenue accounted for a significant portion of the total, but revenue from services (like iCloud and the App Store) was also growing steadily. This diversification in revenue sources is a key strength, as it shows that Apple is not overly reliant on one product.

Next, we look at **Cost of Goods Sold (COGS)**. Apple's COGS for 2023 came in at about $221 billion. This includes all the costs associated with manufacturing its products, from the materials used to make the iPhones and Macs to the assembly costs in various factories around the world. Subtracting COGS from revenue gives us **gross profit**, which for Apple was around $173 billion in 2023. This is the money left after covering the direct costs of making its products and it shows us that Apple has a high gross profit margin—a sign that the company is able to sell its products at a premium and still make a healthy profit.

Now, let's move on to **operating expenses**, which for Apple were about $40 billion in 2023. This covers the costs associated with running the business, including research and development (R&D), marketing, sales and general administrative costs. Subtracting these operating expenses from gross profit gives us **operating profit**, or EBIT, which for Apple was $133 billion in 2023. This figure shows that Apple is efficiently managing its operations, with a significant portion of revenue flowing through to operating profit.

Finally, we reach **net profit**, which for Apple in 2023 was $99 billion. This is the final measure of profitability, taking into account all costs, including interest and taxes. With a net profit margin of 25%, Apple is a highly profitable business—one that's able to generate significant returns for shareholders.

By breaking down Apple's income statement like this, we can see that the company is not only generating substantial revenue, but it's also managing its costs effectively to produce healthy profit margins. For investors, this is a great sign, as it shows that Apple is a well-run, profitable company with a strong potential for continued success.

Understanding the income statement is essential for any investor, especially when evaluating a company's ability to generate sustainable profits. By examining each of these components—revenue, COGS, operating expenses and profit margins—you can start to get a clear picture of a company's financial health. With practice, you'll become more confident in your ability to analyse income statements and use that information to make smarter, more informed investment decisions.

How to Read the Income Statement

When you look at an income statement, you're not just looking at a bunch of numbers thrown together. You're reading the story of a company's financial journey. Each figure on that sheet tells you something about how well the company is doing, where it's spending its money and whether it's making the kind of profits that can lead to long-term success. But how do you make sense of it all?

In this section, we'll take a step-by-step approach to reading and interpreting the figures on an income statement. Understanding revenue and gross profit is essential, as these are the starting points for evaluating the overall health of a business. We'll also look at the difference between operating profit and net profit, as this is where things get a little more nuanced. Finally, we'll explore how to approach the income statement of a small Australian business, taking a more personal, Buffett-style approach to assessing its potential.

Understanding Revenue and Gross Profit

Let's start with the most straightforward parts of an income statement: **revenue** and **gross profit**. These two figures are often the first things an investor looks at and for good reason—they provide essential insights into a company's core operations. But how do you evaluate these figures properly?

Revenue (or sales) is the total amount of money a company earns from selling its products or services. At first glance, a growing revenue figure can seem like a great sign. However, it's important to dig deeper to understand whether that growth is sustainable. A business might report higher revenue, but if it's driven by temporary spikes (like seasonal sales or one-off deals), that doesn't tell you much about its long-term viability. Look at how revenue has trended over time—whether it's growing steadily year after year—or if it's jumping around without consistency. A steady increase in revenue is a strong indicator that a company's products or services are in demand and that the business is positioned well for the future.

But revenue on its own doesn't tell you much about a company's profitability. That's where **gross profit** comes in. Gross profit is calculated by subtracting the **Cost of Goods Sold (COGS)** from revenue. COGS represents the direct costs tied to producing a product or delivering a service. For example, if you run a bakery, your COGS would include the cost of flour, sugar and other ingredients needed to bake the goods. Gross profit shows you how much money is left after covering these direct costs, giving you a better idea of whether the company is operating efficiently.

Here's why gross profit is so important: it reflects the company's ability to control its direct costs and still make a profit. If a company's gross profit margin is consistently high, it's a sign that the business has pricing power (i.e., it can charge a premium for its products) or is good at managing production costs. A low gross profit margin, on the other hand, can signal inefficiencies, poor pricing strategies or rising production costs. To get a real sense of whether a company is in good shape, compare its gross profit margin with those of other companies in the same industry. If a company's margin is higher than its competitors', it's a strong indicator that it's doing something right in terms of cost management or product quality.

Operating Profit vs. Net Profit

Now that you understand revenue and gross profit, let's move to two important figures: **operating profit** and **net profit**. These terms are often used interchangeably, but they actually tell different stories about a company's financial health.

Operating profit, also known as **earnings before interest and tax (EBIT)**, focuses on the profits generated from a company's core business activities. It's calculated by subtracting operating expenses (like wages, rent and marketing costs) from gross profit. What makes operating profit important is that it excludes items such as taxes, interest payments and one-off gains or losses. This gives you a clearer picture of how well the company is doing with its day-to-day operations. Essentially, it shows how much money the company is making from the business it runs, before considering any other financial obligations.

For value investors like Warren Buffett, **operating profit** is often a more reliable indicator than net profit. Why? Because it focuses on the company's operational performance and avoids distortions caused by non-recurring items. For example, a company might sell a large portion of its assets or take on a huge loan, both of which could skew net profit figures. Operating profit, on the other hand, is a purer measure of ongoing profitability, showing whether the core business is healthy and sustainable in the long term.

Then there's **net profit**, which is what most people think of when they hear the word "profit." Net profit is the amount of money the company has left after all costs have been deducted, including taxes, interest and any extraordinary items (such as the sale of assets or restructuring costs). While net profit is certainly important—it's the bottom line of the income statement—it can sometimes be misleading, especially if the company is dealing with one-off events that temporarily boost or reduce profit.

Let's say a company sells an asset for a large gain in a particular quarter. While this might increase net profit, it's not something that will happen regularly. This is why Buffett often favours operating profit over net profit, because it's a clearer reflection of the company's core business performance. If you want to understand whether a company's operations are truly profitable, operating profit is your go-to figure.

Real-life Example: A Small Australian Business

Now that we've covered the theory, let's bring everything together with a real-world example of a small Australian business. Imagine we're looking at a local café in Sydney, called *Sunny's Café*. Sunny's has been growing steadily over the past few years and you want to assess whether it's a good investment opportunity. Here's how we'd approach the income statement from a Buffett-style perspective.

Start with **revenue**. Sunny's Café generates revenue by selling food and drinks and for the year, its revenue is $500,000. That's a solid starting point, but we need to know whether the café is consistently increasing its revenue over time. If last year's revenue was $450,000, the $500,000 this year shows a healthy 11% growth. This is a good sign, but we need to look deeper—how much of this growth comes from increased foot traffic and how much might be due to price hikes or one-off events?

Next, let's look at **Cost of Goods Sold (COGS)**. For Sunny's, COGS includes the cost of ingredients (coffee beans, milk, pastries), as well as packaging and delivery costs. Let's say COGS for the year is $180,000. Subtracting this from revenue gives us **gross profit**, which for Sunny's is $320,000. This tells us that after covering the direct costs of making and selling its food, the café keeps 64% of its revenue as gross profit.

Now, let's move on to **operating expenses**, which include rent, salaries, utilities and marketing. For Sunny's, operating expenses come to $250,000. Subtracting this from the gross profit leaves us with an **operating profit** of $70,000. This is a crucial number because it shows how much money the café is making from its core operations, before accounting for interest, taxes or any unusual events. If Sunny's operating profit margin (operating profit divided by revenue) is around 14%, this is a healthy sign for a small business.

Finally, we look at **net profit**. Let's assume that after paying interest on a small loan and taxes, Sunny's net profit for the year comes to $50,000. This is the final number to consider, but it's important to note that it includes some financial costs that aren't directly related to the café's day-to-day operations.

By looking at Sunny's income statement, we can see that it's a profitable business with steady revenue growth. But the real value comes from understanding the operating profit, which tells us how well the business is running at its core. As Buffett would say, focus on the operating profit to gauge the true health of the business.

Reading an income statement is about more than just understanding the numbers—it's about knowing what those numbers are telling you. By focusing on revenue, gross profit and operating profit and comparing these figures over time, you can get a clear picture of a company's financial health. Whether you're analysing a large corporation like Apple or a small Australian café like Sunny's, these steps are crucial in determining whether a business is worth investing in for the long term.

Analysing the Income Statement

When it comes to evaluating a company's income statement, looking at the raw numbers is only part of the process. To truly understand a company's financial health, you need to dive deeper into the margins—gross, operating and net margins. These margins give you insight into how efficiently a company is running its operations and whether it's positioned for long-term profitability. In this section, we'll explore the importance of profit margins, how they can be used to compare companies and how you can calculate and interpret these margins using real-life examples.

Profit Margins – What Buffett Looks For

One of Warren Buffett's favourite ways to assess a company's financial performance is by looking at its **profit margins**. These margins are key indicators of how well a company is managing its costs and whether it's creating value for shareholders. Understanding the difference between **gross margin, operating margin** and **net margin** will give you a deeper insight into a company's operations and help you spot potential strengths or weaknesses.

Gross margin is the first figure to look at, as it shows how efficiently a company is producing its goods or services. Gross margin is calculated by dividing **gross profit** (revenue minus the cost of goods sold) by **revenue**. For example, if a company generates $1,000,000 in revenue and has $600,000 in COGS, its gross profit is $400,000, and its gross margin would be 40%. A higher gross margin means the company is able to keep a larger percentage of its revenue after covering the direct costs of production. For Buffett, a company with a high and stable gross margin is more attractive because it suggests that the business has pricing power or cost efficiencies that allow it to generate profits more easily.

Next, we have **operating margin**, which takes gross profit a step further by considering operating expenses like salaries, marketing and general administrative costs. Operating margin is calculated by dividing **operating profit** (gross profit minus operating expenses) by **revenue**. This figure helps you understand how well the company is managing its day-to-day operations. A high operating margin indicates that the company is controlling its expenses effectively while generating revenue. For Buffett, companies with strong operating margins are often considered more capable of weathering economic downturns, as they're able to make a profit even when revenue growth slows down.

Finally, there's **net margin**, which shows the company's overall profitability after all expenses, including interest and taxes, have been deducted. Net margin is calculated by dividing **net profit** by **revenue**. While net margin is the most comprehensive measure of profitability, Buffett often focuses more on gross and operating margins because they give a clearer picture of the company's ongoing operational efficiency, excluding external factors like taxes or one-off expenses.

Buffett's strategy is to invest in businesses with strong, consistent profit margins that show the ability to generate profits regardless of market conditions. The goal is to find companies with a durable competitive advantage—businesses that can produce a high margin consistently over the long term. For instance, companies with strong brand recognition, like Coca-Cola or Apple, are often able to command higher prices for their products, leading to better margins. A business with weak margins, on the other hand, might struggle to remain profitable as costs rise or competition intensifies.

Comparing Profitability Across Industries

While profit margins are incredibly useful for understanding a company's performance, they need to be evaluated in context. What's considered a good margin for one company might not be the same for another, particularly when you're comparing companies across different industries.

Take **technology** companies, for example. Companies like Apple, Microsoft and Google typically have very high gross and operating margins, thanks to their ability to sell software, services or high-end devices at a premium price. In contrast, companies in more traditional industries, like **retail** or **manufacturing**, may have lower margins because they deal with higher costs to produce their products or services. A retail company like Woolworths or Coles (Australian supermarket chains), for example, might have lower gross margins because it sells goods that are subject to intense price competition and require a high level of operational expenses, like store rentals and supply chain management.

Buffett uses margins to compare companies within the same industry, as this gives him a more accurate measure of relative performance. A tech company with a 40% operating margin might be doing much better than a competitor with a 10% margin, but in the **retail** sector, a 10% margin could be considered quite healthy. Therefore, it's essential to compare companies within their own industries to gain meaningful insights.

For example, if you're comparing two **Australian** retailers, let's say JB Hi-Fi and Bunnings, their profit margins will give you a clear picture of which company is running more efficiently. A company like JB Hi-Fi, which relies on electronics and appliances, might have lower margins than Bunnings, which sells hardware and home improvement goods. By looking at their margins side by side, you'll be able to determine which one is better at converting its revenue into profit, even if they're operating in the same industry. This kind of comparison helps you make more informed decisions when selecting investments within a specific sector.

Another example can be found in **banks**. Australian banks like Commonwealth Bank or ANZ often have relatively high operating margins because of their steady income from interest on loans and banking fees. When comparing two banks, an investor might look at operating margin to gauge which bank is more efficient at generating profits from its core banking activities. However, the margins of a bank are likely to be different from those of a retail company, so it's important to benchmark each company against similar businesses to get an accurate sense of its profitability.

Practical Exercise: Calculating Profit Margins

Now that you have a good understanding of profit margins and how to interpret them, let's put this knowledge into practice. We'll walk through an example using a small Australian business, **Bobby's Café**, and calculate its key profit margins from its income statement.

Let's say that Bobby's Café has the following figures from its income statement for the year:

- Revenue: $1,200,000
- Cost of Goods Sold (COGS): $600,000

- Operating Expenses: $400,000
- Net Profit: $120,000

We'll calculate the **gross margin, operating margin,** and **net margin.**

Step 1: Calculate Gross Margin

Gross margin tells us how much profit the café is making after covering the direct costs of production, like ingredients and supplies. To calculate it, subtract the COGS from revenue, and then divide by revenue.

- Gross Profit = Revenue − COGS = $1,200,000 − $600,000 = $600,000
- Gross Margin = Gross Profit ÷ Revenue = $600,000 ÷ $1,200,000 = 0.50 or 50%

So, Bobby's Café has a **gross margin of 50%,** meaning that for every dollar of revenue, the café keeps 50 cents after covering the cost of ingredients and supplies. This is a solid margin for a café, indicating that it's managing its direct costs well.

Step 2: Calculate Operating Margin

Next, we calculate the operating margin, which accounts for operating expenses such as rent, utilities, and wages.

- Operating Profit = Gross Profit − Operating Expenses = $600,000 − $400,000 = $200,000

- Operating Margin = Operating Profit ÷ Revenue = $200,000 ÷ $1,200,000 = 0.17 or 17%

Bobby's Café has an **operating margin of 17%**, meaning that after covering all of its operating expenses, the café keeps 17 cents from every dollar of revenue. This is a good margin for a small business, suggesting that Bobby's Café is efficiently managing its operations.

Step 3: Calculate Net Margin

Finally, we calculate the net margin, which takes into account all expenses, including taxes and interest.

- Net Margin = Net Profit ÷ Revenue = $120,000 ÷ $1,200,000 = 0.10 or 10%

The **net margin is 10%**, which means that after all expenses are deducted, Bobby's Café keeps 10 cents from every dollar of revenue as profit. This is a healthy net margin, showing that the café is able to generate profit after covering all of its costs.

By calculating and comparing these profit margins, you can assess Bobby's Café's overall financial health and efficiency. With a strong gross margin, healthy operating margin and a solid net margin, Bobby's Café is running a profitable business. This kind of analysis can be applied to any company, big or small, to help you evaluate its potential for long-term success.

In summary, profit margins are crucial for understanding a company's operational efficiency and profitability. By focusing on gross, operating and net margins, and comparing these figures within industries, you can gain valuable insights into how well a company is performing and whether it has the potential to be a good investment. As you continue practising this analysis, you'll become more adept at spotting strong businesses with sustainable profit potential.

Chapter 1 Summary: Understanding the Income Statement

In this chapter, we've covered the essentials of the **income statement**, a key financial report that shows a company's revenue, expenses and profit over a specific period. We explored the main components: **revenue, Cost of Goods Sold (COGS), operating expenses** and **net profit**, which together provide insight into a company's profitability.

We also looked at **profit margins**—gross, operating and net margins—which help assess how efficiently a company turns revenue into profit. Each margin offers a different perspective, with gross margin focusing on production costs, operating margin including broader expenses and net margin showing the company's final profitability after all expenses.

Finally, we discussed how to compare profit margins across industries. Since margins vary by industry, comparing companies within the same sector helps you understand how they perform relative to one another. A practical example using a small Australian café helped demonstrate how to calculate and interpret profit margins in real life.

Key Takeaways:

- The income statement reveals how a company earns, spends, and profits.

- Profit margins (gross, operating, and net) show how efficiently a company generates profit.

- Comparing profit margins across similar companies helps you gauge performance within an industry.

Reflective Questions:

1. How would you explain the income statement to someone new to investing?

2. After looking at a company's profit margins, how would you assess its operational efficiency?

3. If you were analysing a small business for investment, what key figures in its income statement would you focus on?

Chapter 2: Demystifying the Balance Sheet

What is the Balance Sheet?

When most people think about a company's financial health, they tend to focus on how much money it's making. After all, profit is often seen as the ultimate indicator of success. However, if you're looking at the bigger picture, you need to take a close look at the **balance sheet**. This often-overlooked statement provides a snapshot of a company's financial position at a specific point in time. While the income statement shows the company's ability to generate profit over a period, the balance sheet reveals what it owns, what it owes and the value remaining for shareholders. It's an essential document for anyone looking to understand a company's financial stability and its long-term potential.

Warren Buffett is known for his careful analysis of the balance sheet. To him, the balance sheet is a tool that reveals much more than just numbers; it provides insights into how a company is structured, how it manages debt and how much cushion it has in times of economic stress. For

Buffett, it's not just about what a company owns or owes—it's about understanding whether the company is financially sound enough to withstand challenges and whether it's operating with a level of prudence that he can trust.

The Balance Sheet Defined

The balance sheet is a financial statement that provides a snapshot of a company's financial position at a specific point in time. At its core, it's built on a fundamental accounting equation:

Assets = Liabilities + Equity

This equation is crucial because it shows the relationship between a company's resources (assets), what it owes (liabilities) and the value that belongs to its shareholders (equity). The balance sheet ensures that the company's financial records are balanced, meaning that the company's assets are funded by either debt (liabilities) or by the shareholders' equity.

To simplify it, think of it like this:

- **Assets** represent everything the company owns, such as cash, buildings, inventory and investments.
- **Liabilities** represent what the company owes to others, like loans, bills and other debts.

- **Equity** represents the net worth of the company or what's left for shareholders after all liabilities have been paid off.

Buffett often emphasises the importance of **equity** because it reflects the ownership stake that investors hold in the company. The more solid a company's equity base, the less likely it is to be financially stressed by short-term liabilities. This is why investors like Buffett focus on companies with strong equity positions and manageable debt. A company with a healthy balance sheet and a strong equity base is more likely to weather economic storms and continue growing in the long run.

Buffett's focus on **assets** is also important because assets are the resources a company can use to generate future profits. A company with valuable assets—such as intellectual property, strong brand recognition or physical property—has the potential to create wealth over time. However, he also takes a careful look at liabilities. If a company is burdened with excessive debt, it may struggle to manage its obligations, particularly during tough financial times. For Buffett, it's about finding a balance between assets, liabilities, and equity that signals long-term financial health.

Key Components of the Balance Sheet

A well-structured balance sheet breaks down a company's assets and liabilities into two broad categories: **current** and

non-current. Understanding the difference between these categories is essential for evaluating a company's financial stability.

- **Current assets** are assets that are expected to be converted into cash or used up within a year. These might include cash, accounts receivable (money owed to the company by customers) and inventory. For a company to be financially healthy, it needs to have enough current assets to cover its short-term liabilities, such as accounts payable or short-term debt.

- **Non-current assets**, on the other hand, are long-term assets that are not expected to be turned into cash within a year. These could include property, plant and equipment (like machinery or office buildings), intangible assets (such as patents or trademarks) and long-term investments. Non-current assets are important because they represent a company's ability to generate future value and profits. For a company to be sustainable, its non-current assets should be high-quality and capable of generating returns over time.

Next, we have **current liabilities**, which are debts or obligations that need to be settled within a year. These might include short-term loans, accounts payable (money the company owes to suppliers) and accrued expenses (such as wages or taxes). A company must have enough current assets to cover these short-term obligations, as failing to meet them could lead to liquidity problems.

Then, there are **non-current liabilities**, which are obligations due beyond a year. These could be long-term loans or bonds that the company has issued. While non-current liabilities are generally less urgent than current liabilities, they still represent a significant portion of a company's financial obligations. A company with too much long-term debt may find it difficult to grow or invest in its operations, especially if its cash flow isn't strong enough to service that debt.

Finally, we have **equity**, which is the residual value of a company after all liabilities have been paid off. Equity represents what the shareholders own in the company and it can be thought of as the company's net worth. In simple terms, equity is what's left for the owners after the company's debts are settled. This is an important figure because a high equity base typically suggests that the company is less reliant on debt and more likely to be financially stable.

When you look at a balance sheet, the key is to evaluate whether a company has enough **current assets** to cover its **current liabilities** (this is often referred to as **working capital**). You also need to assess the quality of its **non-current assets** and whether the company's **equity** is strong enough to absorb any financial shocks or downturns.

Real-life Example: Commonwealth Bank of Australia's Balance Sheet

To help bring these concepts to life, let's take a closer look at the balance sheet of the **Commonwealth Bank of Australia** (CBA), one of the largest and most well-known banks in the country. By examining the balance sheet of a major institution like CBA, we can better understand how a value investor like Buffett would approach the analysis.

Looking at CBA's most recent balance sheet, we see that its **total assets** are substantial, amounting to over $1 trillion. Of this, a large portion is made up of **loans** and **investments**, which are considered non-current assets. These assets are key to the bank's profitability, as they generate interest income over time. The **quality of these assets** is critical—if the bank's loans are mostly high-quality (meaning they're likely to be paid back), CBA is in a strong position. On the other hand, if a large portion of its loans are non-performing (meaning the bank is struggling to collect payments), that would be a red flag for investors.

In the **current assets** section, we see things like **cash and cash equivalents**, which give the bank the liquidity to meet its short-term obligations. CBA has a solid amount of cash reserves, which is important for a bank's financial stability. Liquidity is particularly important in the banking sector, as banks need to have enough cash on hand to meet withdrawal demands from customers and cover other immediate expenses.

On the liabilities side, CBA has a mix of **current liabilities** (like short-term borrowings and accounts payable) and **non-current liabilities** (such as long-term debt and bonds). One key figure that Buffett would likely focus on is the **debt-to-equity ratio**, which gives insight into how much debt the bank is carrying compared to its equity. A high debt-to-equity ratio means the bank is more reliant on borrowing to fund its operations, which can be risky in times of economic downturn. In contrast, a lower ratio indicates that the bank has a more solid equity base, which provides a buffer during difficult times.

Finally, in the **equity** section, we see the **shareholders' equity**, which represents the net value of the bank after all debts have been paid off. For a value investor like Buffett, strong equity is a sign that the bank has been able to generate profits over time and is able to reinvest those profits into its operations. The higher the equity, the more financial cushion the company has to withstand economic challenges and grow in the future.

Looking at CBA's balance sheet through Buffett's lens, we can see that the bank has a strong mix of assets, manageable liabilities, and solid equity. This would likely be seen as a good sign for long-term investors, as it suggests that the bank is financially stable and capable of continuing to generate profits, even in uncertain times.

The balance sheet is a powerful tool for assessing the financial health of a company and understanding it is essential for making informed investment decisions. Whether you're looking at a large institution like CBA or a small business, evaluating the assets, liabilities and equity gives you a clearer picture of how the company is structured and whether it's financially sound. By focusing on a company's ability to manage debt, grow its equity and maintain a healthy balance between current and non-current assets, you can make more confident, data-driven investment decisions.

How to Read the Balance Sheet

Now that you understand what the balance sheet is and the key components that make it up, it's time to learn how to read it effectively. When Warren Buffett examines a company's balance sheet, he doesn't just look at the numbers; he digs into the details to understand the quality of its assets, the structure of its liabilities and the overall financial health of the business. In this section, we'll explore how to assess the balance sheet by focusing on two key areas: **assets** and **liabilities**, and how to do this in a way that reflects Buffett's approach. We'll also look at how to apply these insights to a real-world example—a high-growth Australian tech start-up.

Assessing the Asset Side

When evaluating a company's balance sheet, one of the first things Buffett focuses on is the quality and liquidity of its assets. He's not just interested in how many assets a company has, but more importantly, whether those assets are valuable and easily convertible to cash when needed. For Buffett, the quality of a company's assets is crucial because it reflects how well the company can use those resources to generate future profits.

Let's start with **current assets**, which are those likely to be converted into cash or used up within a year. These assets include cash, accounts receivable (money owed by customers) and inventory. For Buffett, **liquidity** is key. He looks for companies with enough **liquid assets** to cover short-term liabilities. This ensures that the business can meet its immediate financial obligations without having to rely on debt or external financing. If a company doesn't have sufficient liquid assets, it may struggle to cover bills or pay off debts, especially in tougher times.

But it's not just about having cash on hand. Buffett also looks at the **quality** of current assets. For example, accounts receivable are only valuable if customers are likely to pay their bills. A company with a large amount of accounts receivable might look healthy on paper, but if those receivables are ageing or customers are unlikely to pay, they could be an unreliable asset. In other words, Buffett would be cautious of companies with a high proportion of receivables that are overdue or difficult to collect.

When it comes to **non-current assets**, such as property, plant and equipment (PP&E), or intangible assets like patents and trademarks, Buffett is looking for **assets that have lasting value**. A strong brand, valuable intellectual property and well-maintained physical assets can be a significant source of future revenue. However, these assets need to be evaluated carefully because they are harder to convert into cash quickly. If a company's PP&E is high but not generating sufficient returns, it may indicate that the company is not using its assets efficiently.

Buffett also focuses on a company's **return on assets (ROA)**, which is a measure of how well a company uses its assets to generate profits. The higher the return on assets, the better the company is at turning its resources into actual profit. A high ROA suggests that the company is effectively utilising its assets to drive earnings, which is a good sign of operational efficiency.

Understanding Liabilities

While assets are essential, you should also place equal importance on understanding a company's **liabilities**, particularly its **debt levels**. One of Buffett's core investment principles is that a company should have **manageable debt**. Companies with excessive debt are at greater risk, particularly in times of economic downturns or when interest rates rise. That's why when Buffett examines a company's balance sheet, he's always looking for businesses that can comfortably meet their obligations without relying too much on borrowed money.

Current liabilities are obligations that need to be settled within a year, such as short-term borrowings, accounts payable (money owed to suppliers) and accrued expenses like taxes and wages. A company needs enough **current assets** to cover these short-term liabilities to ensure it can maintain liquidity. If current liabilities exceed current assets, it can indicate a liquidity problem, where the company might struggle to meet its short-term obligations.

When looking at **non-current liabilities**, which are debts due beyond a year, Buffett's main concern is whether the company can generate enough **cash flow** to meet these obligations. Companies with high non-current liabilities, like long-term loans or bonds, need consistent earnings and solid cash flow to avoid financial distress. If a company is unable to meet its debt payments, it could be forced to borrow more or sell assets, which could impact its future profitability.

One of the best ways to assess debt levels is to look at the **debt-to-equity ratio**. This ratio shows how much debt a company has relative to its equity. A high ratio means that the company relies more heavily on debt to fund its operations, which can be risky, especially in volatile markets. Buffett prefers companies with a low debt-to-equity ratio because they are less dependent on borrowing and more likely to have a stable financial footing.

Buffett's approach to debt is focused on **safety**. He avoids companies that take on too much debt and prefer businesses with strong, manageable liabilities. He often refers to the importance of the "moat"—a business's ability to generate consistent earnings without taking on excessive risk. A company with manageable debt and strong assets is likely to have a moat that can withstand economic uncertainty.

Real-life Example: A High-Growth Australian Tech Start-Up

To put all of this into practice, let's look at the balance sheet of a hypothetical **high-growth Australian tech start-up** called **TechNow**, which specialises in software development for businesses. TechNow is a young, fast-growing company with a lot of potential, but we'll need to evaluate its balance sheet to determine whether it's financially healthy.

First, we look at **current assets**. TechNow has $500,000 in cash, $200,000 in accounts receivable, and $100,000 in inventory. This gives us a total of $800,000 in current assets. On the **liabilities side,** TechNow has $200,000 in current liabilities, which are mostly short-term borrowings to fund operations. This gives TechNow a **current ratio** (current assets divided by current liabilities) of 4.0 ($800,000 ÷ $200,000). A ratio above 1.0 indicates that the company has enough liquid assets to cover its short-term debts and in

TechNow's case, a ratio of 4.0 is a strong indicator of financial stability.

Next, we turn to **non-current assets**. TechNow's biggest non-current asset is its intellectual property (IP), valued at $2 million. The company also owns a small office building worth $500,000. This gives us a total of $2.5 million in non-current assets. Buffett would want to assess the quality of these assets—how valuable and sustainable is the IP? Is it something that can continue to generate revenue for years to come? TechNow's high-value IP suggests that it's in a strong position to generate long-term profits, which is a good sign for future growth.

On the **liabilities side**, TechNow has $1 million in long-term debt. This is a significant portion of its total liabilities and Buffett would carefully consider whether TechNow's future cash flow can comfortably cover this debt. If TechNow's software products continue to grow in demand and generate consistent revenue this debt should be manageable. However, if the company faces slower growth or increasing competition, it might struggle to meet its debt obligations.

When we look at **equity**, TechNow's shareholders' equity stands at $1.3 million, indicating that the company is relatively well-capitalised and not overly reliant on debt. The **debt-to-equity ratio** is approximately 0.77 ($1 million in debt ÷ $1.3 million in equity), which is reasonable and suggests that TechNow isn't overly leveraged.

Buffett would likely view TechNow as a **promising investment**, but he'd want to see continued growth in its revenue and consistent cash flow to ensure that the company can comfortably manage its debt. While the start-up's high-quality intellectual property and manageable debt levels are positive, Buffett would want to monitor its financial performance closely over the next few years to see if it can live up to its potential.

Reading the balance sheet is a key skill for any investor and understanding how to assess a company's **assets** and **liabilities** is crucial for making informed decisions. By focusing on liquidity, quality of assets and manageable debt, you can better assess a company's financial stability and long-term prospects. In the case of TechNow, we've seen how Buffett's approach helps identify a company with good potential but also highlights the importance of continued growth and financial prudence in a high-risk environment. As you gain more experience, these principles will guide you in making more confident investment decisions.

Analysing the Balance Sheet

In this section, we'll take a deeper dive into some of the most important financial metrics that investors like Warren Buffett use when analysing a company's balance sheet: the **debt-to-equity ratio, working capital** and **liquidity ratios**. These metrics help assess the financial health of a company by providing insight into how it is managing its debt and whether it has enough short-term assets to cover its obligations. By the end of this section, you'll have a solid understanding of how to calculate and interpret these ratios, making it easier to evaluate companies, especially when you're looking to make long-term investments.

Debt-to-Equity Ratio – A Key Indicator

Warren Buffett has always been cautious when it comes to companies that rely too heavily on debt. One of his fundamental principles is that **too much debt is dangerous**—especially when market conditions turn unfavourable. The **debt-to-equity ratio** is one of the most important tools for assessing a company's financial leverage (the amount of debt used to finance the company's operations) and its overall risk.

The **debt-to-equity ratio** compares a company's total debt to its shareholders' equity. In simple terms, it tells you how much debt the company is using to finance its operations in relation to the money that has been invested by shareholders. The formula for calculating the debt-to-equity ratio is:

$$Debt-to-Equity\ Ratio = \frac{Total\ Debt}{Shareholders'\ Equity}$$

Buffett's rule of thumb is straightforward: **Avoid companies with high levels of debt**. A company with a high debt-to-equity ratio is more leveraged, meaning it relies more on borrowed money to fund its operations. While some debt is necessary for growth, especially in capital-intensive industries, too much debt can leave a company vulnerable to financial distress if its revenue drops or if interest rates rise.

A **high debt-to-equity ratio** means the company is exposed to more risk. If things go wrong—such as a downturn in the market or a rise in borrowing costs—the company may struggle to pay off its debts, which can lead to financial difficulties. Conversely, a **low debt-to-equity ratio** suggests that the company is relying more on equity (shareholder investment) to fund its operations, which is generally considered a safer bet for long-term stability. Buffett prefers companies with a manageable level of debt—enough to fuel growth but not so much that it risks financial health.

For example, if a company has a debt-to-equity ratio of **2.0**, it means that for every dollar of equity, the company owes two dollars in debt. This could be a sign of heavy reliance on debt, which may raise concerns, especially in uncertain economic times. On the other hand, a ratio of **0.5** means the company has half as much debt as equity, which Buffett would see as more conservative and stable.

Evaluating Working Capital and Liquidity

In addition to understanding a company's debt, Buffett places a strong emphasis on evaluating its **working capital** and **liquidity**. These two metrics help determine whether a company can meet its short-term obligations without running into financial trouble. Working capital is a measure of a company's ability to fund its day-to-day operations, while liquidity refers to the company's ability to quickly convert assets into cash to cover its liabilities.

Working capital is calculated by subtracting **current liabilities** (short-term obligations) from **current assets** (assets that can be converted into cash within a year):

Working Capital = Current Assets − Current Liabilities

A positive working capital means that the company has more current assets than current liabilities, which is a good sign that the company has the financial flexibility to meet its short-term obligations. On the other hand, negative working capital means the company doesn't have enough short-term assets to cover its short-term liabilities, which can be a sign of financial strain.

Buffett focuses on companies with **strong working capital positions** because they are more likely to be financially healthy and capable of sustaining growth. A company with solid working capital can fund its day-to-day operations without relying too heavily on external financing. Strong working capital is particularly important during periods of economic uncertainty, as it ensures that the company has enough resources to continue operating even if revenue fluctuates or cash flow temporarily slows.

Liquidity ratios help assess how easily a company can convert its assets into cash to cover its immediate liabilities. The **current ratio** and the **quick ratio** are the most common liquidity ratios:

- **Current ratio** is calculated by dividing current assets by current liabilities:

$$Current\ Ratio = \frac{Current\ Assets}{Current\ Liabilities}$$

A current ratio above **1.0** indicates that the company has more current assets than current liabilities, meaning it's in a healthy liquidity position. However, if the ratio is much higher than 1.0, it might suggest that the company isn't using its assets efficiently to generate revenue.

- **Quick ratio** is similar but excludes inventory from current assets since inventory may not be as easily converted into cash. The formula is:

$$Quick\ Ratio = \frac{Current\ Assets - Inventory}{Current\ Liabilities}$$

A quick ratio of **1.0** or higher is considered good because it means the company has enough liquid assets (like cash and receivables) to cover its short-term obligations without relying on inventory. For Buffett, a healthy liquidity position is crucial, as it shows that the company can weather short-term financial challenges without being forced to sell assets or take on more debt.

Practical Exercise: Debt-to-Equity and Liquidity Ratios

Now that we've covered the theory behind the debt-to-equity ratio and liquidity ratios, let's apply this to a practical example. Imagine we're analysing the balance sheet of an

Australian retail company, called **RetailCo**, to assess its financial stability. Here are the figures from its latest balance sheet:

- **Current Assets:** $2,000,000
- **Current Liabilities:** $1,200,000
- **Total Debt:** $3,000,000
- **Shareholders' Equity:** $2,500,000

Let's start by calculating the **debt-to-equity ratio** for RetailCo. Using the formula we discussed earlier:

$$Debt-to-Equity\ Ratio = \frac{Total\ Debt}{Shareholders'\ Equity} = \frac{3,000,000}{2,500,000} = 1.2$$

RetailCo's **debt-to-equity ratio is 1.2**, which means that for every dollar of equity, the company has $1.20 in debt. This is a fairly high ratio, indicating that RetailCo relies more heavily on debt to fund its operations. While this might not be a dealbreaker, it suggests that the company is more leveraged and could face challenges if its revenues decline or interest rates rise. Buffett would likely see this as a **cautionary sign** and might prefer companies with a lower ratio, as they are generally less risky.

Next, let's calculate the **current ratio** to assess RetailCo's working capital and liquidity position:

$$Current\ Ratio = \frac{Current\ Assets}{Current\ Liabilities} = \frac{2,000,000}{1,200,000} = 1.67$$

A **current ratio of 1.67** means that RetailCo has $1.67 in current assets for every $1 of current liabilities. This is a healthy ratio, indicating that the company has enough short-term assets to cover its immediate obligations. It suggests that RetailCo is in a **strong liquidity position** and can likely weather any short-term financial challenges without significant issues.

Finally, let's calculate the **quick ratio**, which excludes $500,000 worth of inventory from current assets:

$$Quick\ Ratio = \frac{Current\ Assets - Inventory}{Current\ Liabilities} = \frac{1,500,000}{1,200,000} = 1.25$$

RetailCo's **quick ratio of 1.25** shows that the company has $1.25 in liquid assets (excluding inventory) for every $1 in current liabilities. This is also a strong result, suggesting that RetailCo is not overly reliant on inventory to meet its short-term obligations and has a solid buffer of cash and receivables.

By calculating these ratios, we can see that **RetailCo has manageable debt**, a **healthy liquidity position** and enough working capital to cover its short-term obligations. While the debt-to-equity ratio is a bit higher than Buffett would typically like, the strong current and quick ratios suggest that RetailCo is financially stable in the short term. For Buffett, this might be a company worth keeping an eye on, especially if its debt level decreases over time or if it continues to show strong cash flow and profitability.

Conclusion

In this section, we've learned how to analyse a balance sheet by focusing on key metrics like the **debt-to-equity ratio**, **working capital**, and **liquidity ratios**. These indicators provide crucial insights into a company's financial health and long-term stability. Buffett's focus on companies with manageable debt and strong liquidity positions reflects his cautious and risk-averse investment philosophy. By applying these principles, you can start evaluating companies with a more discerning eye, helping you make more informed investment decisions.

Chapter 2 Summary: Demystifying the Balance Sheet

In this chapter, we've learned how to read and understand the balance sheet, one of the key financial statements every investor should know. The balance sheet provides a snapshot of a company's financial position at a specific moment in time, showing what it owns (assets), what it owes (liabilities) and the value remaining for shareholders (equity). We've explored how Warren Buffett uses the balance sheet to assess a company's financial stability, focusing on important metrics like assets, liabilities and equity.

We also delved into how to evaluate the quality of a company's **assets** and **liabilities**, with a particular emphasis on **debt-to-equity ratios** and **working capital**. Buffett looks for companies with manageable debt and strong liquidity, as these are signs of long-term financial health. Finally, we worked through a practical example, using a high-growth Australian tech start-up, to see how these principles can be applied in real-life scenarios.

Key Takeaways:

- The balance sheet shows a company's financial position by listing assets, liabilities and equity.

- The **debt-to-equity ratio** helps assess how much debt a company is using relative to equity and too much debt can be risky.

- Strong **working capital** and liquidity are essential for a company to meet its short-term obligations and continue operating smoothly.

Reflective Questions:

1. How would you explain the importance of the balance sheet to someone new to investing?

2. After looking at a company's debt-to-equity ratio, what would be your next steps in assessing its financial health?

3. If you were evaluating a start-up, what key aspects of its balance sheet would you focus on to assess its long-term stability?

Chapter 3: Cracking the Cash Flow Statement

What is the Cash Flow Statement?

In the world of investing, a company's ability to generate cash is the lifeblood of its operations. You might hear people say, "cash is king" and for good reason. Unlike profit, which can be affected by accounting choices and estimates, cash flow is a much more reliable measure of a company's financial health. It's one of the reasons why Warren Buffett places so much emphasis on cash flow when evaluating companies. Profit can sometimes be misleading, especially if a company has high non-cash expenses or has recognised revenue prematurely. But cash flow is harder to manipulate and provides a more accurate picture of whether a company is truly thriving.

In this section, we'll break down what the **cash flow statement** is, why it's so important and how you can use it to assess a business's performance. We'll also explore the three main sections of the cash flow statement—**operating activities, investing activities** and **financing activities**—and understand how each section gives us valuable insights into a company's financial health. Finally, we'll use the **cash flow statement of Woolworths**, a major Australian retailer, as a real-world example to see how all of this comes together.

The Importance of Cash Flow

To fully grasp why cash flow is so important, it helps to think about the difference between cash and profit. **Profit**, as we saw in chapter 1, is the difference between what a company earns and what it spends, as reflected in the income statement. However, profit doesn't always tell the full story. A company can show a profit, but if it's not generating enough cash to pay its bills, cover its debts or reinvest in the business, then that profit is a lot less meaningful.

This is where the **cash flow statement** comes in. The cash flow statement tracks the actual cash entering and leaving the company, offering a clear picture of whether the company is generating enough cash to support its operations and growth. Unlike profit, which can be influenced by non-cash accounting items like depreciation or deferred revenue, cash flow is a real-time measure of the company's ability to meet its obligations and create value.

Warren Buffett has always emphasised the importance of **free cash flow**—the cash a company generates after it has paid for capital expenditures (like buying equipment or building new facilities). Free cash flow is important because it tells you whether the company has enough leftover cash to pay dividends, pay down debt, or reinvest in the business. For

Buffett, a company with strong, consistent free cash flow is more likely to be a stable, profitable business in the long run. In contrast, a company with poor cash flow might be relying on borrowing or external financing to stay afloat, which could be a sign of financial instability.

Buffett also prefers companies that can generate cash from their **core operations**. If a company is generating solid cash flow from its operating activities (as opposed to financing or selling assets), it indicates that the business is truly viable and not just dependent on external sources of funds. This is why Buffett looks for companies with **strong operating cash flow**—it's an indicator that the business is fundamentally sound and can sustain itself over time.

Key Components of the Cash Flow Statement

The cash flow statement is divided into three main sections, each of which focuses on a different aspect of the company's cash flows: **operating activities, investing activities**, and **financing activities**. Let's break down each of these sections to understand what they mean and how they can help us assess a business's health.

1. **Operating Activities**: This section is all about the cash generated or used by the company's core operations. It includes cash receipts from customers, cash payments to suppliers, employees, and other operational expenses. The operating section is particularly important because it reflects the

company's ability to generate cash from its day-to-day activities, like selling products or services. A company with positive operating cash flow is generally seen as financially healthy because it shows that the company is able to fund its operations and pay its bills from its core business activities.

Operating cash flow is often seen as a more reliable measure of a company's profitability because it doesn't include one-time items like asset sales or loans. For example, if a company generates a large profit in a quarter but has negative operating cash flow, it could signal that the company is not actually generating cash from its operations and may be at risk of running out of cash.

2. **Investing Activities**: This section includes cash flows related to the purchase and sale of long-term assets, such as property, equipment and investments. If a company is spending money on capital expenditures (CAPEX) to buy new assets or expand its operations, this will be reflected in the investing section. While these outflows may appear as a negative on the cash flow statement, they are often a sign that the company is investing in its future growth.

On the other hand, if a company is selling off assets or investments, this will show up as a positive cash flow in the investing section. However, consistent selling of assets might raise a red flag—it could indicate that the company is struggling to generate cash from operations and is relying on asset sales to stay afloat. Ideally, a company should have a balance of cash outflows for necessary investments in growth and cash inflows from the sale of non-core or non-performing assets.

3. **Financing Activities**: The financing section includes cash flows from raising or repaying capital. This might include borrowing money, issuing or repurchasing stock or paying dividends. Positive cash flow in this section could indicate that the company is raising funds to support its operations or growth, while negative cash flow could suggest that the company is paying down debt or returning money to shareholders.

While financing activities are an important part of a company's cash flow, they should not be relied on as the primary source of funds. A company that regularly relies on borrowing or issuing new equity to fund its operations may not be sustainable in the long term. Buffett is particularly cautious of companies that are constantly raising funds through debt or equity offerings, as it suggests that the company is not generating enough cash from its operations to fund its growth.

Real-life Example: Woolworths' Cash Flow Statement

To put all these concepts into perspective, let's look at a real example using the **cash flow statement** of **Woolworths**, one of Australia's largest and most recognisable retailers. Woolworths operates across supermarkets, liquor stores and various other sectors, making it a prime candidate for us to examine how cash moves in and out of a business with diverse operations. By breaking down its cash flow statement, we can see how the company handles its cash from operating, investing and financing activities.

Let's start with **operating activities**, which, as we discussed, is the heart of any business's cash flow. For Woolworths, the operating section shows a strong **net cash inflow** from its core retail business. This means that Woolworths is able to generate significant cash by selling groceries, liquor and other goods in its stores. In its most recent cash flow statement, the company reported a solid operating cash flow of over **$2 billion**, which is a great sign for any business. This figure reflects the company's ability to turn its sales into actual cash and not just paper profits.

The reason this is so important is that it shows Woolworths is not just profitable on paper—it's actually generating real, usable cash from its core business. For Buffett, this is a critical element in evaluating a business. Many companies can show impressive profits, but if they aren't converting those profits into cash, they could be in trouble. Woolworths, however, seems to have a strong cash conversion cycle, meaning that it's not just relying on profits reported in the income statement but is also able to fund its operations without needing to borrow heavily or rely on other external financing.

Within the operating section, Woolworths' cash receipts from customers are substantial, far outstripping its cash payments to suppliers, employees and taxes. This is typical for a large retailer like Woolworths, but it still shows that the company's core operations are working efficiently. Importantly, the company is managing its working capital well. For example, it's able to collect payments from customers promptly while managing its payables efficiently. This strong cash flow from operations ensures that Woolworths can continue running its stores, paying its suppliers and making sure its shelves are stocked, without having to rely on outside sources of cash.

Next, we look at the **investing activities** section of the cash flow statement. This section shows the company's investments in future growth. Woolworths typically invests a lot of money into improving and expanding its stores, supply chain infrastructure and digital platforms. In its latest cash flow statement, Woolworths reported a **net outflow** of about **$1.3 billion** in investing activities. This is primarily due to its capital expenditures (CAPEX)—money spent on new stores, refurbishing existing stores, investing in its distribution centres and enhancing its online shopping experience.

At first glance, a large cash outflow in investing activities might seem concerning, but for a company like Woolworths, it's actually a positive sign. It shows that the company is reinvesting in its business to fuel future growth. Retail is a competitive industry and to stay ahead, companies must continually improve their physical stores and digital platforms to meet consumer demand. For instance, Woolworths' investment in expanding its delivery network and enhancing its online grocery shopping services has paid off, especially given the increased demand for online shopping in recent years. So while these investments may cause short-term cash outflows, they are likely to generate long-term benefits in the form of higher sales and a larger customer base.

Another aspect of Woolworths' investing activities is its acquisitions. In the past few years, Woolworths has expanded its business through acquisitions, such as the purchase of online delivery businesses and other complementary services. These strategic acquisitions are meant to diversify the company's operations and ensure it can continue competing in the rapidly evolving retail landscape. While acquisitions can lead to immediate cash outflows, they can provide strong returns in the long run if the businesses acquired help drive additional revenue and profits.

Moving on to the **financing activities** section, this part of the cash flow statement reflects how the company is raising and returning capital. For Woolworths, the financing section shows a combination of cash inflows and outflows. For instance, the company has raised funds by issuing bonds or taking on long-term debt, but it has also used some of its cash flow to repay debt and pay dividends to shareholders. In the most recent cash flow statement, Woolworths reported a **net outflow** of around **$500 million** in financing activities, which reflects its focus on paying down debt and returning capital to shareholders in the form of dividends.

Woolworths is known for paying regular dividends, which is attractive to investors looking for consistent income from their holdings. However, it's important to see how the company balances paying dividends with managing its debt. In this case, Woolworths appears to be in a strong enough position to return cash to shareholders while also reducing its debt burden, which is a healthy sign of financial stability. It shows that Woolworths is able to generate enough cash to reward investors without jeopardising its long-term growth prospects.

Looking at these three sections together—operating, investing and financing—we get a clear picture of Woolworths' financial health. The company generates significant cash from its operations, is actively reinvesting in its future growth and is managing its debt and equity in a balanced way. This is exactly the type of business that Warren Buffett would be drawn to. He likes companies that are **cash-generating machines**, able to produce enough free cash flow to reinvest in growth, pay down debt and return value to shareholders, all while maintaining financial stability.

Importantly, Woolworths' strong operating cash flow and strategic investments reflect a business that is well-positioned for the future. Buffett often talks about **moats**, the competitive advantages that allow a company to maintain its market position and generate consistent profits. Woolworths' ability to generate reliable cash flow from its retail operations, combined with its investments in e-commerce and infrastructure, creates a strong moat that will help the company stay competitive in an increasingly digital world.

Conclusion

The cash flow statement is a crucial tool for evaluating the financial health of any company, especially in understanding its ability to generate cash from core operations. Woolworths' cash flow statement shows a business that is not only profitable but also well-positioned to continue growing in the long run. By focusing on operating cash flow, strategic investments and the ability to manage debt, Woolworths is demonstrating strong financial management that will likely support its future success.

For investors, understanding cash flow is vital to making informed decisions. A company might report profits, but if it isn't generating cash from its operations, that could be a warning sign. Woolworths, with its strong cash flow from operations and focus on long-term growth through investment and debt management, represents the kind of business that Warren Buffett looks for—a stable, profitable company with the potential for sustained success. As you continue to study cash flow statements, remember to look for businesses with solid operating cash flow, smart investments and a healthy approach to debt, as these are the signs of a company that's built to last.

How to Read the Cash Flow Statement

Now that we've introduced the importance of the cash flow statement, it's time to dive deeper into how you can read and analyse it. A well-constructed cash flow statement tells you everything you need to know about a company's ability to generate and manage cash. But knowing how to interpret the information is key. In this section, we'll break down how to assess the **operating cash flow**, understand the **role of investing and financing activities** and use **real-world examples** to illustrate these concepts.

Understanding Operating Cash Flow

The first section we'll look at is **operating cash flow**. This is the cash a company generates from its core business operations. It's the lifeblood of any company because it shows how well the business is able to generate cash from selling goods or services. Think of it as the money the company actually takes in after all the normal operations have been carried out, such as paying suppliers, employees and other operating expenses.

Operating cash flow is important because it directly reflects the health of the company's **core business activities**. For instance, if a company is consistently generating strong operating cash flow, it's likely that the business is sustainable and financially sound. However, if a company shows strong profits but negative operating cash flow, this could be a red flag. Profit, after all, can be influenced by accounting methods, such as depreciation or revenue recognition timing, but cash flow gives you a clearer picture of whether the company can actually pay its bills and reinvest in growth.

To determine if a company is generating enough cash from its core business, you need to look at the **operating cash flow figure** in the statement and compare it to its profits. If operating cash flow is higher than net profit, this generally means the company is converting its revenue into cash effectively. On the flip side, if operating cash flow is consistently lower than net profit, it may indicate that the company is struggling to collect its receivables or has too much money tied up in inventory, both of which can create financial strain.

Another important aspect to consider is whether the company's operating cash flow is **sustainable**. For Buffett, sustainability is key. A company that generates consistent and reliable operating cash flow is much more attractive than one that experiences large fluctuations. A business with strong operating cash flow can continue to reinvest in its growth and pay dividends to shareholders without taking on excessive debt or relying on outside funding.

The Role of Investing and Financing Cash Flows

While operating cash flow is crucial, understanding how a company handles its **investing** and **financing activities** is also key. These sections of the cash flow statement show

how the company is using its cash to invest in growth and manage its capital needs.

1. **Investing activities**: This section shows the cash flows related to the purchase and sale of long-term assets, like property, equipment, and investments. For Buffett, the key is not just how much a company is investing, but how wisely those investments are being made. Is the company using its cash to expand its operations and increase its revenue potential? Or is it spending excessively on non-core assets that don't contribute to future profits?

For example, a company might spend a large amount of cash on buying new property, upgrading machinery or acquiring another business. These investments are often positive in the long run, as they can increase the company's capacity for growth and generate more cash in the future. However, if a company is spending a large amount of cash on investments that don't add value to its core operations, this could be a red flag. Buffett is always cautious of companies that appear to be overspending on non-essential acquisitions or investments, especially if those investments aren't likely to produce a good return.

2. **Financing activities**: This section shows the cash flows related to raising capital and paying off debts. Companies raise funds through issuing stock, borrowing money or using other financial instruments. The financing section can show whether a company is relying too heavily on external funding, such as

taking on large amounts of debt or whether it's able to generate enough cash from its core business to support its operations and growth.

For Buffett, it's important that companies have **manageable debt**. If a company is constantly raising money through debt or issuing new shares to fund operations, it may signal that the company isn't generating enough cash from its core activities to sustain itself. Ideally, a company should be able to fund its operations and growth from the cash it generates, rather than relying too much on external financing. When a company uses debt wisely, it can help fuel growth, but excessive borrowing or issuing too many shares can dilute shareholder value or increase financial risk.

Real-life Example: Australian Real Estate Company's Cash Flow

Let's now dive deeper into a real-world example to really see how all these principles come together. We'll take a closer look at the **cash flow statement** of an **Australian real estate company**, which we'll call **AussieHomes**, a major player in property development, investment and management across key Australian cities. AussieHomes develops both residential and commercial properties and has been experiencing rapid growth over the past few years.

Looking at its cash flow statement, we can break down how the company is handling its cash flow from operating activities, investments and financing, and see what this reveals about its financial health.

Operating Cash Flow

When we start with the **operating cash flow**, we see that AussieHomes has generated **$200 million** from its core property development and management activities. This is a very healthy figure, particularly for a company in the real estate industry, where cash flow can sometimes be volatile due to the cyclical nature of property markets. The strong operating cash flow reflects that AussieHomes is able to consistently convert its revenue from property sales and management fees into actual cash.

Operating cash flow is the cash the company generates through its core business activities—selling, leasing and developing properties. For a real estate company like AussieHomes, this section is critical because it tells us whether the company is truly generating cash from its operations or relying on external sources of funding. This $200 million in operating cash flow is a strong signal that AussieHomes is running its day-to-day operations efficiently and that it can meet its financial obligations from its core business without needing to borrow excessively or sell off assets.

However, there are a few things to watch here. A quick look at the **accounts receivable** shows that AussieHomes has **$50 million** outstanding in payments from buyers and tenants. This indicates that while the company is generating cash from its sales and leases, some of that cash is still tied up in unpaid invoices. This is quite typical in the real estate industry, where buyers may take time to settle payments after purchasing properties, but it's also something investors need to monitor. If the company's accounts receivable keep growing without being collected, it could indicate potential liquidity problems down the line.

AussieHomes has managed to keep its **inventory turnover** high, meaning it's not sitting on unsold properties for too long. This is an important point—properties, particularly residential units or commercial buildings, can take time to sell or lease. A company with poor inventory turnover might face higher costs and potentially reduce its cash flow in the future. However, AussieHomes seems to be managing this quite well, selling or leasing a significant portion of its inventory relatively quickly, which bodes well for its cash flow sustainability.

Investing Cash Flow

Next, we look at the **investing activities** section of AussieHomes' cash flow statement. Here, the company has reported a **net outflow of $180 million** due to capital expenditures (CAPEX), as the company continues to invest in new developments and property acquisitions. This spending is mainly going towards purchasing land, constructing new buildings and upgrading existing properties. In the real estate sector, these kinds of investments are crucial because they lay the foundation for future revenue streams.

While a large outflow in the investing section might initially look like a negative, for a property development company like AussieHomes, this is expected. Real estate is a capital-intensive business and investing in land, infrastructure and new buildings is necessary for long-term growth. The key here is whether these investments are generating future value. Woolworths, for example, might invest heavily in expanding its stores, but so too does AussieHomes in expanding its property portfolio. As long as the money is being spent wisely—on properties that are expected to increase in value or generate reliable rental income—this is a positive sign.

However, we also need to note that AussieHomes has also sold some of its existing properties, bringing in **$50 million** in cash. Selling off properties can be a sign that the company is looking to liquidate some assets, but if it's done strategically—such as selling non-core or underperforming assets—it can actually be a good thing. If a company is constantly selling off assets just to raise cash for day-to-day operations, that could indicate a problem with generating cash from its core business. However, in AussieHomes' case, the property sales appear to be part of a broader strategy to reinvest the proceeds into higher-yielding developments.

Buffett would likely focus on how much AussieHomes is spending on **growth** versus how much is being spent on non-strategic areas. If the company were selling properties just to meet short-term obligations, this would raise a red flag. However, AussieHomes' approach seems to involve strategic investments, building new properties in high-demand areas and selling off assets that no longer fit with the company's growth strategy. This is a good example of reinvesting profits into projects that will continue to generate cash flow in the future.

Financing Cash Flow

Now, let's take a look at the **financing activities** section, where we see how AussieHomes is handling its capital needs. This section reports a **net inflow of $120 million**, which comes from **debt issuance**—the company raised money by issuing bonds and taking on long-term loans. This is a common strategy in the real estate sector, where large capital is required to fund development projects. The company also repaid **$40 million** of existing debt, reflecting its commitment to managing its debt load.

From Buffett's perspective, **debt management** is key. He prefers companies that can finance their operations with cash flow from their core business rather than relying too much on debt. For AussieHomes, the **debt-to-equity ratio** is something that should be closely monitored. At this stage, the company seems to be using its debt cautiously. The additional debt raised this year is being used to fund long-term development projects and not just to cover operational costs. This is a good sign because it suggests that AussieHomes is using debt as a tool to fuel growth, rather than simply relying on borrowed money to sustain its business.

Importantly, AussieHomes has also paid out **$30 million** in **dividends** to shareholders. This reflects the company's commitment to returning value to its investors. While paying dividends is a good thing, it's important to remember that a company should only pay out dividends if it has generated enough cash to cover the payments. For AussieHomes, the dividend payments are a sign that the company is generating reliable cash flow and is able to distribute part of that to shareholders, while still maintaining the funds necessary to invest in its future growth.

However, if AussieHomes were paying high dividends while struggling to generate cash from operations, this would be a potential red flag. Buffett prefers companies that can balance returning value to shareholders with reinvesting in growth opportunities. It's clear that AussieHomes is managing this balance well, as it is maintaining a healthy level of debt while still providing returns to its investors.

Conclusion

When you break down AussieHomes' cash flow statement, you see a company that is making intelligent investments in its future while maintaining strong cash flow from its core business. The operating cash flow is robust, showing that AussieHomes is generating enough money from its property development activities to fund operations and future growth. Its investment activities are focused on long-term growth, with capital expenditures directed toward acquiring valuable land and developing new properties. Finally, the company is managing its financing activities prudently, using debt to fund growth while also paying down obligations and rewarding shareholders with dividends.

For investors like Warren Buffett, AussieHomes would appear to be a good example of a company with strong fundamentals. Its ability to generate operating cash flow, wisely invest in its future and manage its capital needs in a balanced way are key indicators that the company is financially sound and positioned for long-term success.

When reading a cash flow statement, keep these principles in mind: operating cash flow shows the strength of the core business, investing activities reveal how the company is positioning itself for the future and financing activities give insight into how the company is managing its capital needs. A healthy balance across these three areas is a good sign that the company is on solid footing. In the case of AussieHomes, the company's cash flow statement indicates it is in a strong position to continue growing and generating value for shareholders.

Analysing the Cash Flow Statement

The cash flow statement is more than just a report on a company's financial movements—it's an essential tool for understanding the health of the business. It reveals how a company is managing its money and provides a clear picture of its ability to generate cash from its operations, fund growth and meet its obligations. In this section, we'll focus on how to analyse the cash flow statement from an investor's perspective. We'll explore **free cash flow**, how to distinguish between **cash flow and profit** and walk through a practical exercise to help you understand how to analyse a company's free cash flow.

Free Cash Flow – Buffett's Favourite Metric

When it comes to analysing cash flow, one of the most important metrics to focus on is **free cash flow (FCF)**. This is one of **Warren Buffett's favourite metrics** and for good reason. Free cash flow is the cash that a company generates from its operations after it has spent the necessary money to maintain or expand its asset base. Essentially, free cash flow tells you how much cash is left over after the company has paid for its capital expenditures (CAPEX), such as purchasing new equipment, upgrading facilities or investing in new projects.

Why does Buffett care so much about free cash flow? For investors, free cash flow is one of the clearest indicators of a company's ability to generate **sustainable** profits and return value to shareholders. A company with healthy and growing free cash flow is in a strong position to reinvest in its business, pay off debt or return money to shareholders through dividends or share buybacks. More importantly, free cash flow shows that the company is able to generate cash from its core business, without relying on external financing or selling assets to fund its operations.

To calculate free cash flow, you start with **operating cash flow** (the cash generated by the company's core business activities), and subtract **capital expenditures (CAPEX)**, which represent the company's investments in long-term assets. The formula looks like this:

$Free\ Cash\ Flow = Operating\ Cash\ Flow - Capital\ Expenditures$

For example, if a company generates $200 million in operating cash flow but spends $80 million on capital expenditures, its free cash flow would be $120 million. This means the company has $120 million in cash left over after funding its necessary investments.

Buffett loves companies with strong, growing free cash flow because it indicates that the business is not only profitable but also financially stable. With free cash flow, a company can weather economic downturns, invest in future growth and even return value to shareholders without having to take on excessive debt or issue new equity.

The key point here is sustainability. Free cash flow is a measure of the company's ability to continue generating cash over time, and it's a critical indicator of long-term financial health. If a company's free cash flow is inconsistent or negative, it might be a warning sign that the business is struggling to generate cash from its operations or is overspending on growth without the returns to justify it.

Cash Flow vs. Profit – What to Trust

One of the most important things to understand when analysing a company's financial statements is the difference between **cash flow** and **profit**. These two terms are often used interchangeably, but they tell very different stories about a company's financial health. Profit, as shown in the **income statement**, is a measure of the company's earnings after expenses, taxes and other deductions. However, profit doesn't always reflect the actual cash the company has available to use for its operations or investments. This is where cash flow comes in.

Cash flow is a more reliable measure of a company's ability to generate money because it tracks the actual movement of cash—whether it's coming in or going out. Profit, on the other hand, can be manipulated by various accounting methods. For example, a company might recognise revenue before it's actually received (a practice known as **accrual accounting**) or it might use **depreciation** to spread the cost of assets over time. These accounting choices can make a company's profit look better than it actually is in terms of cash generation.

Cash flow, particularly **operating cash flow**, provides a clearer picture of whether the company is truly generating cash from its day-to-day activities. For example, a company might show a healthy profit on the income statement but have negative operating cash flow. This would suggest that the company is not actually able to convert its sales into cash and might be relying on borrowing, asset sales or other non-operating sources of funds to stay afloat.

Warren Buffett is particularly cautious about companies with high profits but poor cash flow. Even if a company is reporting high earnings, if it's not able to generate enough cash to cover its operations and growth, the business may be in trouble. For example, if a company is recognising large amounts of revenue but is not receiving the cash from its customers or clients, this could signal potential liquidity issues down the line. Similarly, a company might have high depreciation expenses that lower its reported profit, but depreciation is a non-cash expense, so the company could still be generating cash.

In short, while **profit** can give a snapshot of a company's financial performance, **cash flow** provides a more accurate reflection of its ability to manage its money and sustain its operations in the long run. As Buffett often says, "You can't eat an income statement." It's the cash flow that keeps the business running, pays the bills, and supports future growth.

Practical Exercise: Analysing Free Cash Flow

Let's take these concepts and apply them to a **real-life example** to see how you would analyse free cash flow. For this exercise, let's use an Australian company—**Australian Manufacturing Group (AMG)**, a leading producer of industrial machinery. We'll walk through the steps of analysing AMG's **free cash flow** based on the company's latest cash flow statement.

Step 1: Find the Operating Cash Flow

The first thing you need to do is find the company's **operating cash flow**. This is usually listed in the cash flow statement under the section called **Cash Flow from Operating Activities**. For AMG, the operating cash flow for the year is **$50 million**. This figure shows that AMG is able to generate $50 million in cash from its core business operations, which is a good start.

Step 2: Identify Capital Expenditures (CAPEX)

Next, you need to identify the company's **capital expenditures (CAPEX)**, which represent the money spent on buying, upgrading or maintaining long-term assets like property, equipment or machinery. This is usually listed in the **investing activities** section of the cash flow statement. For AMG, the company has spent **$30 million** on CAPEX during the year, primarily to purchase new machinery and expand its production facilities.

Step 3: Calculate Free Cash Flow

Now, we can calculate AMG's **free cash flow** using the formula we discussed earlier:

Free Cash Flow = Operating Cash Flow − Capital Expenditures

Substituting in the figures from AMG's cash flow statement:

$$Free\ Cash\ Flow = 50\ million - 30\ million = 20\ million$$

So, AMG's **free cash flow** is **$20 million**. This means that after spending money on maintaining and growing its asset base, AMG has $20 million in cash left over. This is a good sign because it shows that the company is generating enough cash from its core operations to support its growth, pay down debt and potentially return value to shareholders in the future.

Step 4: Evaluate the Free Cash Flow

Now that we've calculated AMG's free cash flow, let's take a moment to evaluate it. A free cash flow of $20 million is a solid result, but it's important to assess it in the context of AMG's business and industry. For a manufacturing company, a healthy free cash flow allows it to reinvest in new machinery, pay off any outstanding debts or even pay dividends to shareholders. If AMG can continue to generate free cash flow at this level, it will be in a strong position to grow, even in tougher economic conditions.

Buffett would likely look at this figure and ask whether AMG's free cash flow is sustainable. Is the company's business model strong enough to generate reliable cash flow in the long run? Is the $30 million in capital expenditures likely to lead to higher revenue and profits in the future? If the company is investing in growth opportunities that will lead to increased cash generation, then the free cash flow figure will be even more valuable.

Conclusion

When it comes to analysing a company's financial health, **free cash flow** is one of the most important metrics to focus on. It shows how much cash a company is generating from its core business after accounting for necessary investments in growth and maintenance. Buffett's preference for companies with strong, sustainable free cash flow is grounded in the fact that free cash flow is a reliable indicator of a company's ability to reinvest in its operations, pay down debt and return value to shareholders.

By following the steps outlined in this chapter, you can begin to analyse free cash flow for any company, looking at both the operating cash flow and capital expenditures to see how much cash the company is generating and whether it's able to sustain its growth. In the case of **Australian Manufacturing Group**, we saw that the company's ability to generate free cash flow is a positive sign of financial stability and long-term growth potential.

Ultimately, free cash flow helps you determine whether a company is truly generating wealth or just reporting profits on paper. By focusing on this metric, you can make more informed investment decisions, identifying businesses that are truly creating long-term value.

Chapter 3 Summary: Cracking the Cash Flow Statement

In this chapter, we've explored the cash flow statement, one of the most important tools in assessing a company's financial health. We discussed how the cash flow statement is divided into three sections: **operating activities, investing activities** and **financing activities**, each revealing different aspects of a company's cash flow. We also examined the significance of **free cash flow**, a key metric Warren Buffett relies on to assess a company's ability to generate cash after necessary investments and why it's essential for long-term investors.

We also looked at the difference between **cash flow** and **profit**. While profit can be influenced by accounting methods, cash flow provides a clearer picture of how well a company is managing its money and whether it's able to sustain its operations, fund growth and meet financial obligations. The chapter also included a practical exercise, walking through the analysis of **free cash flow** using an example of an Australian company.

Key Takeaways:

- **Free cash flow** is a crucial metric that shows how much cash a company has left after it has made the necessary investments to maintain or grow its business.

- **Cash flow** is more reliable than profit, as it reflects actual cash movements, providing a clearer picture of

- a company's ability to generate and manage its money.
- The three sections of the cash flow statement—operating, investing and financing—offer a comprehensive view of a company's cash flow and financial health.

Reflective Questions:

1. How can you differentiate between cash flow and profit, and why is cash flow a more reliable indicator of a company's financial health?

2. Why is **free cash flow** so important when assessing whether a company is financially stable in the long run?

3. When analysing a company's cash flow statement, what red flags might you look for in the **investing** or **financing** sections?

Chapter 4: Warren Buffett's Key Ratios and Metrics

In this chapter, we'll dive into four key ratios that Warren Buffett swears by when deciding which businesses to invest in for the long haul. These ratios—**Price-to-Earnings (P/E) Ratio, Return on Equity (ROE), Return on Capital (ROC),** and **Earnings Growth Rate**—are the tools Buffett uses to figure out if a company is underpriced, how well it's using its resources and whether it has what it takes to grow steadily over time. Throughout this chapter, we'll break down each ratio, using real-world examples to make these concepts clear and easy to grasp. By the end, you'll understand how Buffett applies these ratios in his investment decisions and how you can use them too.

Price-to-Earnings (P/E) Ratio

One of the most commonly used metrics in the investment world is the **Price-to-Earnings (P/E) ratio** and for good reason. It's a quick way to get a snapshot of how the market values a company relative to its earnings. As a beginner investor, understanding the P/E ratio is key to assessing whether a stock is fairly priced or if it's over- or undervalued. In this section, we will break down what the P/E ratio measures, why Warren Buffett values it and some of its limitations. Along the way, we'll use real-life examples to bring the concept to life.

Defining the P/E Ratio

The P/E ratio is calculated by dividing the company's **share price** by its **earnings per share (EPS)**. Simply put, it shows how much investors are willing to pay for each dollar of the company's earnings. Here's the basic formula:

$$P/E\ Ratio = \frac{Price\ per\ Share}{Earning\ per\ Share\ (EPS)}$$

For example, if **Coca-Cola** has a share price of $60 and an earnings per share (EPS) of $3, the P/E ratio would be:

$$P/E\ Ratio = \frac{Price\ per\ Share}{Earning\ per\ Share\ (EPS)} = \frac{60}{3} = 20$$

This means investors are willing to pay 20 times the company's earnings for each share of Coca-Cola stock. Now, what does this tell us? On a basic level, a **high P/E ratio** often suggests that investors expect future growth and are willing to pay a premium for the stock today. A **low P/E ratio** might indicate that the market perceives the company as having lower growth potential, or it could be undervalued.

Practical Example: Coca-Cola's P/E Ratio

To help put this into context, let's take **Coca-Cola**, one of the world's largest and most well-known brands, as an example. If we look at Coca-Cola's P/E ratio over time, we can see how its valuation compares to its earnings and what investors were willing to pay for those earnings. If the P/E ratio of Coca-Cola is significantly higher than that of its competitors, this could suggest that the market has high expectations for Coca-Cola's future growth or it's perceived as a safer, more reliable investment.

For instance, if Coca-Cola's P/E ratio is 20, and its main competitor, PepsiCo, has a P/E of 15, it may mean that Coca-Cola's stock is more expensive relative to its earnings. Investors might be paying a premium for Coca-Cola based on its dominant market position, brand strength and stability, or it could mean that Coca-Cola has higher growth prospects than PepsiCo in the eyes of the market. Conversely, a lower P/E ratio could mean that Coca-Cola is underpriced relative to its earnings potential, making it an attractive buy.

Why Buffett Uses the P/E Ratio

For Warren Buffett, the P/E ratio is an important valuation tool, but it's not the only metric he uses. He sees the P/E ratio as a helpful starting point for assessing whether a company's stock is overpriced or underpriced. Buffett's investment philosophy is built on buying businesses that he believes are undervalued—stocks that can deliver consistent earnings growth over the long term.

When Buffett evaluates the P/E ratio, he's trying to understand if the market is overvaluing or undervaluing the business. A **high P/E ratio** often suggests that investors expect higher future growth and thus, they're willing to pay more for the stock today. However, a high P/E ratio can also signal **overvaluation** if the company's growth prospects don't justify the premium price.

For another example, let's consider **Amazon**—a company that has been one of the market's most expensive stocks for years, often with a P/E ratio well above 100. When Amazon was in its early growth stages, its P/E ratio was often very high because investors believed that Amazon had the potential to dominate not only retail but also cloud computing, entertainment and other industries. But a P/E ratio of 100+ doesn't necessarily mean that Amazon was a bad investment—it just means that investors were willing to pay a lot for a company they believed had enormous growth potential.

Buffett, however, would be cautious about buying a stock with such a high P/E ratio unless the growth prospects were well-supported by solid fundamentals, a strong business model and the ability to generate profits over the long run. In Amazon's case, its profitability over time has justified its high valuation—allowing the company to grow into its P/E ratio. However, Buffett would have likely scrutinised the company's potential to achieve sustainable profits before making a decision, focusing on whether Amazon could continue to grow at the rates expected by the market.

Practical Example: Amazon's Historical P/E Ratio

Taking Amazon again as an example, its P/E ratio fluctuated dramatically over the years. In its early stages, when Amazon was heavily reinvesting profits into expansion, its P/E ratio was astronomical, reflecting high expectations of future growth. Buffett, who is typically more conservative when it comes to buying high-growth stocks, might have been hesitant at those times, as the market was pricing in significant future success.

However, as Amazon grew and began to show its ability to generate consistent profits—especially after its success with Amazon Web Services (AWS) and global expansion—the market adjusted its expectations and Amazon's stock price gradually aligned with its earnings potential. This transition shows how the P/E ratio can help investors assess whether a company's stock is priced in line with its earnings growth, and whether it's likely to maintain or exceed those expectations.

Limitations and Comparisons

While the P/E ratio is a valuable tool, it is far from perfect. As a standalone metric, it doesn't provide the full picture of a company's financial health or future prospects. **Limitations** of the P/E ratio include the fact that it doesn't account for **debt levels**, **cash flow** or the **quality of earnings**. Additionally, comparing the P/E ratio across different industries can be misleading, as some sectors naturally have higher or lower average P/E ratios.

For example, industries like **technology** or **biotech** often have much higher P/E ratios than traditional industries like **utilities** or **manufacturing**. This is because technology companies, especially those with high growth potential, are typically valued more highly by investors. But, a **high P/E ratio** in one industry doesn't automatically mean the stock is overpriced—it's important to look at the broader context, including industry growth rates and future prospects.

In Buffett's case, he doesn't make decisions based solely on the P/E ratio. He uses it as a starting point but always compares it to other factors—like **earnings growth**, **competitive advantage** and **profit margins**—to ensure that the stock offers good value for the long-term. He focuses more on **sustainable growth** rather than short-term market fluctuations. So, while the P/E ratio is helpful, it's not the be-all and end-all.

Practical Example: Apple's P/E Ratio Over Time

Let's look at **Apple's** P/E ratio over the years to understand how context can change the interpretation of the ratio. For years, Apple was considered a "growth stock" and its P/E ratio was relatively high compared to the broader market.

However, as Apple matured, its P/E ratio began to stabilise, and it shifted from being a growth stock to a more established, value-oriented company. This evolution in Apple's P/E ratio reflects the shift from a high-growth company investing heavily in new markets to a more mature company generating consistent cash flow from its established product lines, like the iPhone.

For Buffett, Apple's consistent ability to generate strong earnings and profit margins, along with its ability to reinvest cash into new growth opportunities (like services and wearables), made its P/E ratio more justifiable over time. What Buffett would have looked at was whether the P/E ratio was sustainable given Apple's potential for ongoing growth in its core business and beyond.

Conclusion

The **P/E ratio** is one of the most commonly used financial metrics, and it provides valuable insights into a company's stock valuation relative to its earnings. For Warren Buffett, the P/E ratio is just one tool in a broader toolkit of ratios and metrics he uses to assess a company's financial health. While it can indicate whether a stock is overvalued or undervalued, it's crucial to take into account other factors, such as **earnings growth**, **debt levels** and the company's **competitive advantage**, before making investment decisions.

Buffett uses the P/E ratio to get a sense of whether a stock is trading at a reasonable price relative to its earnings potential. However, he also considers the broader market conditions, industry trends, and long-term prospects to determine if a company offers true value. Understanding how to interpret and use the P/E ratio, along with other financial metrics, is essential for any investor looking to make informed, long-term investment decisions.

Next time you look at a company, use the P/E ratio as your starting point, but don't forget to ask: What's the company's future growth potential? How does it compare to competitors? And importantly, does the company have the ability to sustain growth over the long run? By applying the P/E ratio alongside these questions, you'll be well on your way to identifying high-quality investments.

Return on Equity (ROE)

What is ROE and How to Calculate It?

Return on Equity (ROE)—one of Warren Buffett's favourite metrics for assessing a company's profitability. Put simply, ROE tells you how effectively a company is using its shareholders' equity to generate profit. If a company is using its investors' money wisely, the ROE will be high, which is a sign of strong management and operational efficiency.

The formula for calculating ROE is straightforward:

$$ROE = \frac{Net\ Income}{Shareholders'\ Equity}$$

To explain this with a practical example, let's take **Woolworths**, one of Australia's biggest supermarket chains. If Woolworths reports a **net income** of $2 billion and has **shareholders' equity** of $8 billion, the ROE would be:

$$ROE = \frac{2\ billion}{8\ billion} = 25\%$$

This means that for every dollar of equity invested in the company, Woolworths generates 25 cents of profit. Not bad, right?

But why is this useful? Well, the higher the ROE, the more profit the company is making with the money its shareholders have invested. For Woolworths, an ROE of 25% suggests it's highly efficient in generating profits. It also shows that the company is able to create value without needing massive amounts of capital.

When we compare this ROE to industry averages, it gives us context. In a capital-intensive industry like retail, a high ROE can be an indicator of a competitive edge, efficient operations or pricing power. If Woolworths' competitors are showing an ROE of 10% or less, we'd see that Woolworths is doing a better job of generating profit from its shareholders' equity.

Why ROE is a Buffett Favourite

Now that we understand what ROE is and how it's calculated, let's look at why Buffett loves this metric so much. For Buffett, a **high and sustainable ROE** signals that the company is efficiently using the capital it has. But more than that, it's a sign of good management. Great managers know how to maximise the returns on the company's capital, and they can do so year after year.

When you see a company with a consistently high ROE, it often indicates a competitive advantage—a kind of moat—that allows the company to operate efficiently, reinvest profits and still grow without relying heavily on external financing. This is exactly what Buffett is looking for. The more efficiently a company uses its equity to generate profits, the more attractive it becomes to an investor like Buffett.

Take **BHP Group**, one of the world's largest mining companies, as an example. If BHP reports an **ROE of 30%**, it shows that the company is generating a significant amount of profit with its equity. This high ROE might be reflective of the company's competitive advantage—perhaps its global scale, strong resource base, and cost efficiencies.

A high ROE like this suggests that BHP's management is skilled at generating returns from the company's capital, which is something Buffett values deeply. For Buffett, a business that can consistently generate high returns on its capital will likely continue to grow without needing to take on excessive debt or issue more equity to fund expansion.

When Buffett finds companies with high, sustainable ROE, he sees them as businesses with the potential to generate long-term wealth for shareholders. These companies are able to reinvest their profits into further growth or pay down debt, creating a positive cycle of profitability.

What to Look for in ROE

Although ROE is a powerful metric, it's important to use it carefully. A very high ROE can sometimes be a red flag if it's being driven by **excessive debt**. Debt can artificially inflate ROE, so it's important to understand how a company is achieving its high return.

For example, a company might borrow heavily to finance its operations, and this increased debt load can boost its ROE because the company has less equity but is still generating profits. This could give a false sense of profitability, as the company's high ROE is a result of its reliance on borrowed funds, not necessarily on its efficiency or competitive edge.

Let's use **Commonwealth Bank of Australia (CBA)** as an example. Suppose CBA has a **high ROE of 18%**. On the surface, this looks good, but if the company is holding a significant amount of debt, the high ROE might be due to leveraging—using borrowed money to generate higher returns. It's important to look at CBA's **debt-to-equity ratio** to see if its high ROE is sustainable or if it's just a result of riskier borrowing.

In cases where debt is a factor, Buffett will often dig deeper. While Buffett isn't necessarily opposed to debt, he prefers businesses that can generate strong returns without relying heavily on borrowing. A high ROE achieved with high debt could be a **warning sign** that the company is more vulnerable to economic downturns or interest rate increases, which could negatively affect its profitability.

It's not just about a high ROE—it's about **sustainable, efficient returns** that come from a strong business model. That's what Buffett is looking for. He's less concerned with short-term spikes in profitability and more focused on companies that can consistently generate high returns over the long run.

Practical Example: Commonwealth Bank of Australia

To bring this point home, let's take a closer look at **Commonwealth Bank of Australia (CBA)**. Over the years, CBA has been one of Australia's most profitable banks and its **ROE** has consistently been strong. However, during periods where the bank has increased its leverage (i.e., taking on more debt), its ROE may rise sharply. Buffett would look at these periods carefully to assess whether the high ROE is sustainable or if it's being driven by too much debt. If CBA can continue to generate its strong ROE without relying on excessive borrowing, it becomes a more attractive investment.

Buffett would want to see that CBA's profitability is coming from its core operations and not from leveraging debt. If the ROE is high and sustainable, backed by a strong business model, he would likely see CBA as a solid investment. But if the high ROE is masking deeper issues—like too much debt or a weakening competitive position—Buffett would probably steer clear.

Conclusion

In this section, we've learned that **Return on Equity (ROE)** is a powerful indicator of how efficiently a company uses its shareholders' capital to generate profits. For Buffett, a high and sustainable ROE is a sign of strong management and a solid competitive advantage. However, it's essential to dive deeper into a company's capital structure to ensure that its high ROE isn't being artificially inflated by excessive debt.

As an investor, you want to look for companies with a consistent ability to generate strong returns from their equity without relying on risky borrowing. A high ROE that comes from sound business fundamentals is a strong indicator of a company's ability to grow and generate value for shareholders over time.

By understanding how to interpret ROE and using it in conjunction with other ratios, you'll be able to assess whether a company is a solid, long-term investment, just like Buffett does. Keep in mind that while ROE is a critical metric, it's most useful when considered alongside other financial metrics, such as debt levels and profit margins, to paint a complete picture of a company's financial health.

Return on Capital (ROC)

What is ROC and Why It Matters

When evaluating a company's financial health, **Return on Capital (ROC)** is a critical metric for understanding how well a business is using all of its resources—both **debt** and **equity**—to generate profits. Unlike **Return on Equity (ROE)**, which focuses only on shareholders' equity, ROC provides a broader view by measuring the efficiency with which a company is using all its capital to create returns. This makes ROC an especially important metric for assessing the overall financial health and profitability of a company, providing a clearer picture of how well a company is generating profit from the total capital it has at its disposal.

$$ROC = \frac{EBIT}{Total\ Capital}$$

Where **EBIT** stands for **Earnings Before Interest and Taxes**, and **total capital** includes both debt and equity. This means ROC looks at how efficiently a company is deploying both its own equity and any borrowed funds (debt) to generate profits.

Let's take **Qantas Airways** as a practical example. Imagine Qantas reports **EBIT** of $1 billion and its **total capital**—which includes both debt and equity—amounts to $10 billion. The ROC would be:

$$ROC = \frac{1\ billion}{10\ billion} = 10\%$$

This means Qantas generates 10% in earnings for every dollar of capital it uses, which is a solid return. By evaluating the ROC, investors can see whether the company is making the most out of the money it has available, whether borrowed or from shareholders. For a company like Qantas, which operates in a highly capital-intensive industry, a solid ROC indicates that it is managing its capital effectively to generate profit, despite the massive costs involved in running an airline.

Why Buffett Uses ROC for Long-Term Investment

For Warren Buffett, **Return on Capital (ROC)** is one of the most important measures of a company's ability to sustain long-term growth without relying on excessive debt. Companies with **high and sustainable ROC** tend to have strong business models, operational efficiencies and competitive advantages that allow them to generate consistent profits without taking on too much debt or needing to raise more capital constantly. This is exactly what Buffett looks for in a company when considering it as a long-term investment.

Buffett's investment philosophy is rooted in **capital allocation**—the ability of a company's management to use its capital effectively to generate returns for shareholders. High ROC indicates that a company's management is doing a good job of deploying the resources at its disposal to produce value. Buffett is drawn to companies that generate solid returns on their invested capital over time because they tend to exhibit characteristics of **economic moats**—sustainable competitive advantages that protect them from competition and enable them to generate high returns in the long term.

Let's look at **Telstra**, one of Australia's largest telecommunications companies, to illustrate this concept. If Telstra has a **ROC of 18%**, it means that for every dollar of capital the company uses—whether it's debt or equity—it is generating 18 cents in profit. For Buffett, this is an attractive number because it shows that Telstra is able to efficiently use its capital to generate consistent returns and it has a competitive edge in the industry.

Now, compare this to a company with a **lower or declining ROC**. A company like that may still be profitable, but if its ROC is decreasing, it may signal inefficiencies, increased competition or a diminishing competitive advantage. This would cause Buffett to be more cautious, as businesses with **declining ROC** might struggle to sustain long-term profitability.

In the case of Telstra, Buffett would likely see the company's solid and stable ROC as a sign of its ability to maintain profits without needing excessive debt. This would make Telstra a company Buffett could confidently invest in for the long term, knowing that it is efficiently managing its resources.

Comparing ROC Across Industries

It's important to note that **ROC varies across industries**. Some industries naturally have higher returns on capital due to lower capital expenditures, while others require heavy investments in physical assets or infrastructure, which can result in lower ROC. Understanding these industry differences is key to evaluating whether a company's ROC is good for its specific sector.

For example, industries like **technology** and **consumer goods** tend to have higher ROC because they often require less capital to generate profits. In contrast, **capital-intensive industries** like **utilities, telecommunications**, and **mining** typically have lower ROC due to the significant investments required in infrastructure, machinery and other assets.

Let's look at a **real-life example: Fisher & Paykel Healthcare**, a leading healthcare company in New Zealand, has historically posted a **strong ROC**. In its sector, which includes developing medical devices and technologies, the capital required to generate profits is relatively low compared to industries like mining or infrastructure development. As a result, Fisher & Paykel is able to achieve a high return on its invested capital, indicating that the company is very efficient in generating profits from its capital.

Now, let's compare this with a company in the **mining sector** like **Rio Tinto**. The mining industry is much more capital-intensive because it requires significant investment in machinery, land and extraction facilities. Therefore, a company like Rio Tinto may have a **lower ROC** compared to Fisher & Paykel, but that's not necessarily a bad sign. In fact, a lower ROC in this context could still be considered strong if the company is generating solid profits from its significant capital investment.

So, comparing ROC across industries helps investors understand whether a company is performing well within the context of its sector. While technology companies tend to have higher ROC, it's more about **relative performance within an industry**. A company with higher ROC than its peers is likely more efficient, while a company with lower ROC might be struggling to generate profits relative to its capital.

Practical Example: Fisher & Paykel Healthcare vs. Rio Tinto

To bring this comparison to life, consider **Fisher & Paykel Healthcare** and **Rio Tinto**. Fisher & Paykel is a relatively high-margin business because its medical devices and equipment require less physical infrastructure, allowing it to generate higher returns on its capital. On the other hand, **Rio Tinto**, a mining giant, requires enormous capital investments in mining operations, which results in a lower ROC but is expected given the high costs associated with extracting and processing minerals.

So, what's important here is the **industry context**. A high ROC in a low-capital industry like healthcare is a positive sign of management's efficiency, but a relatively low ROC in a capital-heavy industry like mining doesn't necessarily signal poor management—it's simply a reflection of the industry's high capital requirements.

Buffett would understand that a high ROC in a capital-intensive industry isn't always as realistic or sustainable as it would be in a less capital-heavy industry. Therefore, it's crucial to compare a company's ROC with that of its competitors and industry peers to see if it's performing well relative to industry norms.

Conclusion

In this section, we've explored **Return on Capital (ROC)**, a crucial metric that reveals how well a company uses all of its capital (debt and equity) to generate profits. For Buffett, a high and sustainable ROC is a sign of a strong, efficient business that can generate long-term value without over-relying on debt. Companies with high ROC often have a competitive advantage, allowing them to produce consistent returns on invested capital.

However, it's also important to understand that ROC can vary significantly across industries. Capital-intensive industries like mining or utilities tend to have lower ROC, while technology and healthcare companies often have higher ROC. By comparing ROC across companies within the same industry, you'll get a clearer sense of how well a company is performing relative to its competitors.

Buffett uses ROC as one of the key indicators to determine whether a company is efficient at allocating capital and whether it has the potential to provide long-term growth. When evaluating a company, always consider the context of its industry and how well it is managing its capital to generate profits. By focusing on high, sustainable ROC, you can identify businesses that are likely to thrive over the long term.

Earnings Growth Rate

Understanding Earnings Growth Rate

The **Earnings Growth Rate** is a critical metric for investors like Warren Buffett because it measures how well a company's earnings are growing over time. More specifically, it tells us the annual rate at which a company's earnings per share (EPS) have increased over a set period—often five or ten years. What Buffett looks for is **consistent, sustainable earnings growth**. He is not interested in companies that experience short-term, speculative earnings spikes; rather, he focuses on companies that can maintain steady, reliable growth year after year.

When a company consistently grows its earnings, it signals to Buffett that the business is fundamentally strong, with a solid competitive advantage and is likely to continue generating value for shareholders. Whether a company operates in **technology, healthcare** or **consumer goods**, reliable earnings growth is often a sign of long-term demand for the company's products or services, and it builds investor confidence.

Let's take **CSL Limited**, an Australian global biotechnology company, as an example. Over the years, CSL has shown impressive and steady earnings growth. This growth is a result of the strong demand for its blood-plasma products, its ability to innovate in the healthcare space and its expanding global market reach. Buffett would see CSL's **earnings growth rate** as a reliable indicator of its potential to continue growing and generating profits for years to come.

For instance, CSL's consistent earnings growth, underpinned by its leadership in the biotechnology sector and its continued investment in research and development, is a good example of the kind of company Buffett seeks. It demonstrates a strong business model, long-term growth potential and a sustainable market position—all qualities Buffett values when making long-term investments.

Why Earnings Growth is Crucial for Buffett's Strategy

While Buffett is not typically drawn to high-growth, speculative stocks, he is highly focused on companies with **strong and predictable earnings growth**. For him, growth should come from sound business fundamentals, not from hype or market trends. In other words, he wants businesses that can increase their earnings in a **reliable and sustainable manner**. He avoids companies whose growth is based on speculative factors or unrealistic projections, as these companies are more likely to face volatile earnings that could lead to poor investment outcomes.

Buffett's investment strategy revolves around identifying businesses with the **ability to grow earnings steadily over time**. Companies with predictable earnings growth tend to have more **stable stock prices**, which aligns with Buffett's preference for **long-term value** over short-term speculation.

Take **Amcor**, an Australian packaging company, as an example. While Amcor may not be as high-growth as a tech start-up, its consistent earnings growth over decades is exactly the type of business Buffett would invest in. The company operates in the packaging sector, which has long-term demand driven by industries such as food, pharmaceuticals and consumer goods. Amcor's ability to consistently increase earnings, through innovation in sustainable packaging solutions and expansion into emerging markets, would signal to Buffett that the company is likely to provide stable returns over the long term.

Buffett's approach to earnings growth focuses on the quality of the growth. He avoids the temptation of buying into companies with **unrealistically high earnings expectations**, which are often tied to speculative or unpredictable factors. Instead, Buffett prefers companies that are able to **increase earnings consistently through solid operational practices**, not through market hype or unsustainable trends.

How to Calculate and Assess Earnings Growth

To calculate earnings growth, you need to look at a company's **earnings per share (EPS)** over a certain period—usually five or ten years. By comparing the current EPS to the EPS from a few years ago, you can calculate the **annual growth rate**. The formula for calculating the earnings growth rate is as follows:

$$Earnings\ Growth\ Rate = \left(\frac{Current\ EPS}{EPS\ from\ N\ Years\ Ago}\right)^{\frac{1}{N}} - 1$$

Where **N** is the number of years you're looking at.

For example, let's say **Santos Ltd.**, an Australian energy company, reported an EPS of $1.00 five years ago and its current EPS is $1.50. The earnings growth rate would be:

$$Earnings\ Growth\ Rate = \left(\frac{1.50}{1.00}\right)^{\frac{1}{5}} - 1 = 8.45\%$$

This means that **Santos' earnings** have grown at an average annual rate of 8.45% over the last five years.

Using a Financial Calculator or Online Calculator

For those who prefer a quicker and easier method than manual calculation, you can use a **financial calculator** or an **online calculator** to determine the earnings growth rate. Here's a step-by-step guide for both:

Using a Financial Calculator (TI BA II Plus as an example):

1. **Turn on your calculator:** Press the **ON** button.
2. **Enter the starting EPS (EPS from N years ago):** For Santos, this would be $1.00.
    - Type **1.00**, then press **Enter**.
3. **Enter the ending EPS (Current EPS):** For Santos, this would be $1.50.
    - Type **1.50**, then press **Enter**.
4. **Enter the number of years (N):** This is 5 years for our example.
    - Type **5**, then press the **N** button.
5. **Calculate the Earnings Growth Rate:**
    - Press the **CPT** button (short for compute), followed by the **I/Y** button (interest per year).

6. The result will be the **Earnings Growth Rate** for the period.

For Santos, the answer should be around **8.45%**.

Using an Online Calculator or App:

If you prefer using an online tool, here's how you can do it:

1. **Search for an online compound interest calculator or app**. Many apps and websites offer free calculators that can compute growth rates.

2. **Enter the initial EPS (EPS from N years ago)**: In this case, type in **$1.00**.

3. **Enter the final EPS (Current EPS)**: For Santos, type in **$1.50**.

4. **Enter the number of years (N)**: This will be **5 years** for our example.

5. **Press "Calculate"** or "Compute" to get the growth rate.

The calculator will instantly provide the **8.45% growth rate**, just like we calculated manually. These tools can save you time and help you perform quick calculations when you're assessing multiple companies.

Buffett is particularly interested in understanding whether this earnings growth is **sustainable**. Sustainable growth comes from strong demand for a company's products or services, effective cost management and the ability to reinvest profits into new growth opportunities.

However, Buffett doesn't just look at the numbers—he also considers the **quality of the growth**. Is the growth coming from sustainable sources, like expanding market share, increasing prices or improving efficiency? Or is it driven by **one-off events**, like acquisitions, which may not be repeatable?

When assessing **Santos Ltd.**, for example, Buffett would look at the broader energy sector, future demand for fossil fuels, and the company's ability to maintain a competitive edge as the world transitions towards more sustainable energy solutions. He'd also consider whether the company's growth is largely driven by new energy projects or acquisitions that may not provide sustained earnings growth.

Santos has recently been focusing on transitioning to more sustainable energy sources and if this shift is creating a reliable, long-term growth trajectory, Buffett would likely see it as a positive sign. However, if Santos' growth was merely driven by fluctuating commodity prices or non-recurring events, it might not be as attractive from Buffett's perspective.

Conclusion

In this section, we've explored the **Earnings Growth Rate**, a crucial metric for evaluating a company's ability to grow its earnings consistently over time. For Buffett, earnings growth is not about **speculative booms** or **short-term market trends**—it's about finding businesses with predictable, **sustainable growth** driven by sound business fundamentals.

By examining a company's earnings growth rate, you can get a clearer sense of whether the business is truly increasing its profitability or if the growth is driven by unsustainable factors. For Buffett, steady earnings growth signals a **strong business model**, a **competitive advantage** and **long-term value**, which are the key attributes he looks for when making investment decisions.

When calculating and assessing earnings growth, always consider the quality of that growth—whether it's driven by genuine, ongoing demand and operational improvements or by one-time factors like acquisitions. Sustainable earnings growth is one of the key pillars of Buffett's strategy and understanding how to calculate and assess it is vital for any investor looking to make informed, long-term investment decisions.

By applying the Earnings Growth Rate alongside other key metrics, you'll have the tools to assess whether a company is likely to deliver consistent returns over time, just like Buffett does.

Chapter 4 Summary: Warren Buffett's Key Ratios and Metrics

In this chapter, we've explored four important financial metrics that Warren Buffett uses to evaluate businesses: **Price-to-Earnings (P/E) Ratio, Return on Equity (ROE), Return on Capital (ROC)** and **Earnings Growth Rate**. Each of these ratios plays a crucial role in helping Buffett assess whether a company is fairly valued, efficiently managed and capable of sustaining long-term growth.

The **P/E ratio** helps gauge a company's valuation relative to its earnings, while **ROE** measures how effectively a company uses its equity to generate profits. **ROC** gives a broader picture by evaluating how well a company uses both its equity and debt to create value. Finally, the **Earnings Growth Rate** highlights a company's ability to grow its profits over time, an important sign of future stability and success.

Buffett's approach to investing is grounded in finding companies with high, sustainable returns, a strong competitive advantage and a reasonable valuation. By mastering these ratios, you'll be better equipped to evaluate companies in a similar way and make informed, long-term investment decisions.

Key Takeaways:

- The **P/E ratio** helps determine whether a stock is overpriced or undervalued relative to its earnings potential.

- **ROE** shows how well a company is using shareholders' equity to generate profit, with higher ROE often indicating efficient management.

- **ROC** provides insight into how effectively a company is using both debt and equity to generate returns and is key to evaluating overall capital efficiency.

- **Earnings Growth Rate** measures a company's ability to grow its earnings consistently, a vital factor for long-term success.

Reflective Questions:

1. How does the P/E ratio help you assess whether a stock is fairly valued and what other factors should you consider alongside it?

2. Why is **Return on Equity (ROE)** such a powerful indicator of a company's efficiency and what might a high ROE reveal about a company's financial strategy?

3. How can you apply the **Earnings Growth Rate** to evaluate a company's future potential and what are

the risks of relying on one-off growth events for long-term success?

Chapter 5: Financial Manipulation and Red Flags

Creative Accounting Examples

When you look at financial statements, it's important to remember that numbers can sometimes be manipulated to tell a different story. Creative accounting is a term that refers to the use of accounting tricks to either present a more favourable picture of a company's financial health or to hide certain problems. Unfortunately, creative accounting can often mislead investors and lead to disastrous outcomes, as it masks the true financial state of a company.

In this section, we'll examine some infamous examples of creative accounting, starting with **Enron's** use of off-balance-sheet entities. We'll then look at how tech companies sometimes manipulate revenue recognition and finish with a real-life case from Australia where a company was caught in questionable accounting practices.

Enron's Use of Off-Balance-Sheet Entities

Let's start with one of the most well-known cases of financial manipulation—**Enron**. In the early 2000s, Enron was hailed as one of the most innovative companies in the world, revolutionising the energy sector. However, the company's spectacular fall from grace exposed massive accounting fraud that ultimately led to its bankruptcy.

One of the primary methods Enron used to hide its debt and inflate its profits was through the use of **off-balance-sheet entities**. These were special purpose entities (SPEs) or partnerships that were created for the sole purpose of keeping debt off Enron's balance sheet. The idea was simple: by moving liabilities to these separate entities, Enron could keep its financial statements looking much cleaner than they actually were. By not reporting the debt, Enron gave the illusion of being more financially stable than it really was.

The company used these entities to hide billions of dollars in debt, which made its financial position look much better than it actually was. When Enron's stock price soared, it became the darling of investors, all while the company was piling on more and more debt in these off-balance-sheet structures. The problem was that, although these debts were kept hidden, they still existed and would eventually come due.

When the truth came out, it was disastrous. Enron's stock collapsed, investors lost billions and the company was forced to declare bankruptcy. This case is a clear example of how creative accounting can be used to hide the reality of a company's financial situation, leaving investors with a false sense of security. It also highlights the importance of thoroughly examining a company's balance sheet and looking for any signs that they might be using creative accounting to hide liabilities or inflate earnings.

Revenue Recognition Issues in Tech Companies

Moving on from Enron, let's look at a different kind of manipulation—**revenue recognition**—which is particularly common in tech companies. Revenue recognition is the process of recognising sales in a company's financial statements and it plays a key role in determining a company's profitability. For many tech companies, especially those with subscription-based services or long-term contracts, recognising revenue at the right time can be tricky. However, some companies have taken advantage of this by recognising revenue too early, which can inflate their earnings and mislead investors.

One common trick is to recognise revenue before it has actually been earned. For example, a company might recognise the full value of a contract in the period in which it signs the deal, even though the service or product hasn't yet been delivered. This creates an immediate bump in revenue but doesn't accurately reflect the actual performance of the company. In some cases, revenue recognition can even occur before the product or service is fully provided, creating a situation where the company reports higher profits than it actually generated.

A classic example of this is **Worldcom**, which used aggressive accounting practices to inflate its earnings in the late 1990s and early 2000s. Worldcom falsely recognised revenue by booking line costs as capital expenses and by inflating the amount of revenue it recognised from customers. This manipulation ultimately led to one of the largest accounting scandals in U.S. history, causing billions of dollars in losses for investors.

In the tech industry, companies like **Cisco** and **Microsoft** have also faced scrutiny over their revenue recognition practices. The temptation to recognise revenue too early is particularly high in the tech world, where businesses often operate on long-term contracts and the pace of innovation is rapid. However, when companies book revenue prematurely, it distorts the financial picture and can mislead investors into thinking the business is performing better than it actually is.

As an investor, it's important to be aware of a company's revenue recognition practices. One way to spot potential issues is to look at the company's **cash flow statement**. If a company reports strong profits but weak cash flow, it may be a sign that it is recognising revenue too early or not collecting cash for sales in a timely manner.

Real-life Case Study: Another Australian Company

While Enron and Worldcom are two of the most infamous examples of financial manipulation, it's also important to look at local companies, especially in Australia, where similar issues have surfaced. Let's take a closer look at a real-life example of an Australian company that was caught using questionable accounting practices.

In 2018, **Corporate Travel Management (CTM)**, an Australian travel management company, found itself embroiled in a scandal involving **overstated revenue**. CTM had been inflating its earnings to meet market expectations, which had led to a misrepresentation of its true financial health. The company was recognising revenue from contracts in a way that did not reflect the actual value of the business, and this gave investors a false sense of the company's profitability.

CTM's use of creative accounting became evident when the company's auditors, after conducting a thorough review, found discrepancies between the revenue the company had reported and the actual revenue generated from its contracts. The company had been booking some of its earnings prematurely, which led to a significant overstatement of its profits. This case is a reminder that even companies listed on the Australian Stock Exchange are not immune to creative accounting practices and it highlights the importance of looking beyond the surface of financial statements to fully understand a company's financial health.

When CTM's manipulation was uncovered, the company's stock price plummeted and its reputation took a massive hit. This case serves as a cautionary tale for investors, showing how financial manipulation can distort the true value of a company and lead to significant losses. It also reinforces the idea that it's not just enough to read a company's profit and loss statement or balance sheet—you must also carefully scrutinise their revenue recognition practices and other accounting policies to ensure that the numbers reflect the true financial picture.

Conclusion

Creative accounting can be a dangerous game. Whether it's Enron hiding its debt through off-balance-sheet entities, tech companies recognising revenue too early or even Australian companies like Corporate Travel Management overstating their earnings, the potential for manipulation is always present. As an investor, it's crucial to understand how companies can manipulate their financials and what red flags to look for.

One of the key lessons from these examples is the importance of **scrutinising a company's financial statements**—especially their revenue recognition practices. If something seems too good to be true or if a company's reported earnings don't match its cash flow, it's worth digging deeper to uncover potential financial mismanagement.

By learning from the mistakes of others and being mindful of the tactics companies use to manipulate their numbers, you can better protect yourself from falling into the trap of investing in companies that are not as financially healthy as they appear. Always remember, when it comes to financial statements, it's not just about looking at the numbers—it's about understanding how those numbers are made and whether they genuinely reflect the company's performance.

Red Flags in Financial Reporting

When you're evaluating a company, it's essential to look for potential **red flags** in its financial reporting. These are signs that something might not be right with the company's operations or financial health and they often indicate underlying issues that could lead to problems down the road. In this section, we'll dive into three common red flags to watch out for: **inconsistent revenue growth**, **unusual changes in liabilities** and **high or increasing days sales outstanding (DSO)**. These red flags can help you spot trouble before it becomes a bigger issue, saving you from making poor investment decisions.

Inconsistent Revenue Growth

One of the first things most investors look at when assessing a company's financial health is **revenue**. After all, if a company can't consistently grow its top line, it's going to struggle to generate profits, reinvest in its business or pay dividends to shareholders. So when revenue growth becomes **inconsistent**, it should raise a red flag.

Sudden spikes in revenue, in particular, can be a sign of trouble. While it's normal for a company to have occasional peaks in revenue, a sharp and unexpected jump often indicates that something is not sustainable. This could be due to a one-off event, like a large sale or an acquisition, that temporarily boosts the numbers. However, if these spikes are repeated or not supported by real growth in the business, it could indicate **manipulation of revenue**—such as recognising revenue too early or inflating earnings.

Take, for example, **Wirecard**, a German payment processing company that became embroiled in a massive fraud scandal. For years, Wirecard reported impressive revenue growth and its stock price soared as a result. However, a closer inspection revealed that much of the revenue growth was not backed by actual sales but by fraudulent transactions and accounting tricks. When Wirecard's manipulations were uncovered, its stock collapsed and investors suffered massive losses.

For Australian investors, one company that also showed **sudden and unsustainable revenue growth** was **Centro Properties Group**, an Australian retail property group. The company was consistently reporting high revenue growth, which seemed healthy on the surface. However, when the company ran into trouble and its books were scrutinised more closely, it was revealed that some of the revenue was being recognised prematurely or based on overly optimistic assumptions. This resulted in the company facing significant financial difficulties, which ultimately led to its collapse in 2011.

So, when you spot sudden spikes in a company's revenue, make sure to **ask why**. Is it sustainable? Are there one-off events driving it? And most importantly, is it supported by real growth in customers, sales and market demand, or is it based on questionable accounting practices?

Unusual Changes in Liabilities

Another major red flag to watch out for is **unusual changes in liabilities**—especially when a company suddenly increases its long-term or short-term debt. Liabilities represent the money a company owes to others and they are an essential part of understanding a company's financial health. However, an increase in debt can signal potential problems. Here's why:

Debt can be a useful tool for companies to finance growth and expansion. However, when a company takes on too much debt, it can become a liability in itself. The ability to service that debt (i.e. paying it off with interest) can become increasingly difficult if the company's revenue starts to slow down or if it faces unexpected financial pressures. An increase in debt, especially if it's **not matched by a corresponding increase in revenue or assets**, can signal that the company is borrowing to cover its losses or is under financial stress.

Take **Australia's ABC Learning Centres**, a childcare provider, as an example. In the years leading up to its collapse in 2008, the company took on a massive amount of debt to fuel its rapid expansion. While the company's revenue appeared to be growing, much of that growth was financed through borrowed money. Eventually, when the company couldn't generate enough income to service its debt, ABC Learning Centres went bankrupt, leaving investors with significant losses.

When looking at a company's balance sheet, watch for any **unusual changes in liabilities**, especially if the company's debt is increasing rapidly without a clear explanation. **Why is the company borrowing more?** Is it to fund a legitimate expansion or is it a sign of deeper financial issues? These are critical questions that could help you spot a company in trouble before it's too late.

High and Increasing Days Sales Outstanding (DSO)

Lastly, **Days Sales Outstanding (DSO)** is a vital metric to keep an eye on. DSO measures the average number of days it takes for a company to collect payment from its customers after a sale. In simple terms, it's a way to gauge the effectiveness of a company's collections process. A **high or increasing DSO** is a **red flag** because it can indicate that the company is struggling to collect payments or is offering more lenient credit terms to customers in order to drive sales.

A **high DSO** can be a sign that the company is experiencing cash flow problems, as it may be waiting too long to receive money from its customers. If customers are slow to pay, the company might have trouble meeting its own financial obligations, such as paying suppliers, servicing debt or funding operations. In the worst case, this could lead to liquidity issues, where the company doesn't have enough cash on hand to keep things running.

For example, in the case of **Helloworld Travel**, an Australian travel agency, its DSO was high and increasing, which was a major red flag for investors. The company was relying on extended credit terms to drive more sales, but as a result, it was taking longer and longer to collect payments from customers. While this strategy might have seemed effective in the short term, it led to significant cash flow issues in the long run, which contributed to the company's financial troubles.

Buffett is particularly cautious about companies with rising DSO, as it signals potential cash flow problems and indicates that the company might not be managing its receivables efficiently. High or increasing DSO can also be a sign that a company is facing issues with customer retention, or it could mean that customers are experiencing financial difficulties and are taking longer to pay their bills.

As an investor, it's important to keep an eye on DSO. If a company's DSO is increasing over time, it's worth digging deeper into its **collections process, credit policies** and **customer base**. Is the company facing problems with collections? Are its customers struggling to pay their bills? These could all point to potential cash flow challenges down the line.

Conclusion

When you're evaluating a company, understanding and spotting red flags in its financial reporting is just as important as assessing its profitability and growth potential. **Inconsistent revenue growth, unusual changes in liabilities** and **high or increasing DSO** are all critical warning signs that can indicate trouble ahead.

The key takeaway here is that **numbers don't always tell the full story**. While financial statements are incredibly important, they can also be manipulated or used in ways that hide underlying problems. As an investor, your job is to look beyond the surface and ask the right questions. If a company's numbers seem too good to be true, or if there are sudden changes that don't make sense, it's important to investigate further.

By being vigilant about these red flags, you can better protect yourself from falling into the trap of investing in companies with hidden financial issues. Always ask yourself: **Why is this happening? What's driving this change?** and **Is it**

sustainable in the long term? These questions will help you spot red flags early and make more informed, smarter investment decisions.

How to Spot Red Flags

In this section, we will explore how to spot **red flags** in a company's financial statements before they become a serious issue. As we've seen in previous examples, financial manipulation or problems in a company's finances often manifest in subtle ways. If you can learn to identify these warning signs early, you'll be in a better position to make informed investment decisions.

Here, we'll break down how to **analyse financial statements for red flags**, understand when something is a cause for concern versus a normal part of business, and go through a **practical exercise** where you can practice identifying these issues using real-world examples. By the end of this section, you'll have the tools to become a more critical and effective investor.

Analysing Financial Statements for Red Flags

The first step in spotting red flags is knowing **where to look** in the financial statements. A company's financial health is reflected in three key documents: the **income statement**, the **balance sheet**, and the **cash flow statement**. Each of these can reveal signs of trouble if you know what to look for.

- **Income Statement**: This statement tells you whether the company is making a profit or loss. Red flags to look for here include **inconsistent revenue growth** or **unusual spikes in profit** that aren't supported by business fundamentals. For example, if a company reports large profits in a quarter but there's little change in sales or customer activity, it might be a sign that profits are being inflated through accounting tricks.

- **Balance Sheet**: The balance sheet shows the company's assets, liabilities, and shareholders' equity. Pay close attention to any **rapid increase in debt** or **decline in cash reserves**. If liabilities are growing faster than assets, this could signal financial instability. A large increase in **off-balance-sheet items** could also be a red flag, especially if the company is hiding debt or obligations that aren't immediately visible.

- **Cash Flow Statement**: The cash flow statement is one of the most revealing documents because it shows how much actual cash the company is generating. A **positive net income** on the income statement paired with a **negative cash flow** is a serious red flag. This could indicate that the company is reporting profits through accounting methods, but not actually collecting cash from its customers or operations.

When you examine these statements, look for any **discrepancies** or trends that don't align with the company's reported financial health. For example, if a company reports significant revenue growth but has weak cash flow, this may indicate problems in collections or issues with customer credit.

Let's use **Aristocrat Leisure** (an Australian company) as an example. Suppose Aristocrat shows strong sales growth in its income statement, but its **cash flow statement** shows declining cash flow from operations. This could be a sign that the company is booking sales but is struggling to collect payments, which could create liquidity issues down the road.

Understanding What to Ignore vs. What to Worry About

Not every anomaly in a financial statement should be considered a red flag. As investors, it's important to understand what **can be ignored** and what needs closer scrutiny. Some variations in financial statements are perfectly normal and part of the company's natural business cycle, while others indicate deeper issues.

Here are some examples of things that **may not need concern**:

- **Fluctuations in Quarterly Earnings**: It's common for companies to have **quarterly fluctuations** in earnings due to seasonality, changes in customer demand, or specific one-off expenses. For instance, a retailer might report lower earnings in the first quarter because of slower post-holiday sales, but this doesn't necessarily indicate a deeper problem. However, **consistent decline** in earnings over several quarters should raise concerns.

- **Changes in Inventory Levels**: Inventory levels can fluctuate due to changes in production cycles or supply chain issues. While a **temporary increase in inventory** could be a sign of slowing sales, it might simply reflect an effort to prepare for a future spike in demand, especially in industries that rely on long lead times for production.

However, there are certain things that **shouldn't be ignored**, such as:

- **Sudden Changes in Debt**: A **rapid increase in debt**, especially without an obvious business reason, is a red flag. If a company takes on a large amount of debt but doesn't have an immediate plan to use it for expansion or operations, this could be a sign that the company is struggling to maintain operations or finance its growth.

- **Unusual Revenue Recognition Practices**: If a company is recognising revenue too early or using aggressive accounting methods, this could indicate that profits are being inflated. Look for companies that recognise **revenue before it's actually earned**, especially in industries where sales are tied to long-term contracts or projects.

- **Unexplained Executive Compensation**: Excessive executive compensation, especially when a company is not performing well, can be a red flag. If senior executives are receiving large bonuses or stock options despite poor company performance, this might suggest that the company is misaligned with shareholder interests.

Understanding the difference between normal and concerning anomalies helps you avoid panicking over every fluctuation, while also ensuring you don't overlook real risks.

Practical Exercise: Identifying Red Flags

Now that we've covered how to spot potential red flags and what to worry about, let's dive into a **practical exercise** to help solidify these concepts. We'll use a real-world company, **Santos Ltd.**, an Australian energy company, to walk through the process of identifying red flags.

Step 1: Examine the Income Statement

Start by looking at Santos's income statement. Pay attention to the **revenue growth** over the last several quarters or years. Is it consistent, or do you see any sudden spikes or drops in revenue?

If you see a sudden spike, check if it aligns with any one-time events—like a large project or acquisition—or if the spike is something that can be explained by the company's normal business cycle. If the spike seems out of place, it could indicate aggressive revenue recognition.

Step 2: Look at the Balance Sheet

Next, take a look at Santos's balance sheet, focusing on **liabilities**. Has the company taken on more debt recently? Is the debt primarily long-term or short-term?

If you see an increase in short-term debt, it could be a red flag that the company is struggling to cover its current liabilities and might face liquidity issues. However, if the increase is in long-term debt for expansion or infrastructure projects, it may be justified, especially if the company's revenue and profits are expected to grow in the future.

Step 3: Examine the Cash Flow Statement

Finally, check out Santos's **cash flow statement**. Compare its **net income** with its **cash flow from operations**. Are they aligned, or is there a large difference? A large gap between net income and cash flow is a red flag, as it might indicate that the company is recognising revenue that it hasn't yet collected in cash.

In this case, if you see a lot of revenue recognised but not a lot of cash flow from operations, it could signal problems with collections or sales quality.

Step 4: Assess DSO (Days Sales Outstanding)

Look at Santos's **DSO**—the average number of days it takes for the company to collect payment from its customers. An increasing DSO could be a sign of trouble, as it means the company is waiting longer to receive cash from its sales. If DSO is rising, it may indicate problems with collections, which could put stress on the company's cash flow.

Conclusion

In this section, we've learned how to spot red flags in financial reporting and how to separate genuine concerns from normal business fluctuations. By closely analysing a company's **income statement**, **balance sheet**, and **cash flow statement** and understanding the difference between anomalies that can be ignored and those that require further investigation, you'll be better equipped to identify potential issues before they escalate.

The practical exercise with Santos Ltd. helps bring these concepts to life. By actively reviewing a company's financial statements, you'll develop the skills needed to spot trouble early. Remember, the more you practice these techniques, the more adept you'll become at recognising the subtle signs of financial manipulation or mismanagement, allowing you to make more informed investment decisions. Always keep an eye on the big picture and don't be afraid to dig deeper if something doesn't seem quite right.

Chapter 5 Summary: Financial Manipulation and Red Flags

In this chapter, we've explored the darker side of financial reporting—**creative accounting** and **red flags**. We looked at real-life examples of companies that used questionable accounting practices, like **Enron's off-balance-sheet entities, revenue recognition issues in tech companies** and a case from an Australian company, **Corporate Travel Management**. These examples show how companies can manipulate financials to give a false picture of their health, leading investors astray.

We also covered common **red flags** to watch for when analysing a company's financial statements, including **inconsistent revenue growth, unusual changes in liabilities** and **high or increasing DSO**. By understanding these warning signs, you'll be better prepared to spot potential issues before they become major problems.

Finally, we provided a practical exercise to help you apply what you've learned by analysing a real-world company's financials, giving you hands-on experience with identifying red flags.

Key Takeaways:

- **Creative accounting** can hide the true financial state of a company, as seen in cases like Enron and Corporate Travel Management.

- **Red flags** like inconsistent revenue growth, rising liabilities and increasing DSO should raise concern and prompt further investigation.

- Always dig deeper into a company's financial statements to understand if there are underlying issues that could affect its long-term health and profitability.

Reflective Questions:

1. What are the key signs that a company might be manipulating its financial statements and how can you spot them early?

2. How can inconsistent revenue growth be a red flag, and what does it indicate about the company's financial health?

3. How would you assess whether an increase in a company's liabilities is a cause for concern or a part of a normal business cycle?

Conclusion: Bringing It All Together

As we wrap up this journey through the world of financial statements, it's time to take a step back and reflect on the key lessons we've covered. Understanding how to evaluate a company's financial health is an essential skill for anyone looking to invest wisely. By mastering the three core financial statements—**the income statement**, **the balance sheet** and **the cash flow statement**—you can begin to build a clearer picture of how a company operates, how it generates and uses money and whether it's a solid investment.

Throughout this book, we've gone through the basics of each statement, identified key metrics like **profit margins**, **ROE**, **P/E ratios**, and **free cash flow** and explored real-world examples to bring these concepts to life. We've also covered the risks of creative accounting and how to spot potential red flags, giving you the tools to make better, more informed decisions when assessing companies.

Now, let's take a moment to recap what we've learned, review a final checklist to guide your evaluations and look ahead at how to apply these lessons in real-world investment decisions.

Summary of Key Learnings

At the core of every financial analysis are three fundamental statements: the **income statement**, the **balance sheet** and the **cash flow statement**. Each of these documents offers a unique insight into a company's operations and overall financial health, and when used together, they provide a comprehensive view of a company's performance.

The **income statement** is the first place to start. It provides an overview of the company's profitability, showing how much revenue it has generated, the costs incurred and ultimately the profit or loss. Key metrics here, like **profit margins** and **operating income**, allow you to see how efficiently the company is operating and whether it is generating enough profit from its sales. We also discussed how to assess **revenue growth** and the importance of spotting any **inconsistent spikes**, which could signal that the numbers aren't quite as healthy as they seem.

Next, we dived into the **balance sheet**, which gives us a snapshot of the company's financial position at a specific point in time. It shows what the company owns (assets), what it owes (liabilities) and the value of shareholders' equity. One of the most important ratios here is the **debt-to-equity ratio**, which helps you determine whether the company is over-leveraged. A manageable level of debt allows a company to grow without taking on excessive risk, while too much debt can signal potential trouble ahead.

Finally, we looked at the **cash flow statement**, which reveals the company's ability to generate cash from its operations, invest in growth, and pay off its debts. It's not just about the profits on paper; it's about the actual cash a company can bring in. **Free cash flow** is a critical metric here and when a company has strong free cash flow, it's better equipped to weather economic downturns, reinvest in its business or return value to shareholders.

When used together, these statements give you a complete picture of a company's financial health. A healthy company should show a balance of strong profitability, manageable debt levels and good cash flow generation. If any one of these elements is missing or looks shaky, it's time to dig deeper.

Final Checklist

Before you dive into the numbers for any company, keep this **final checklist** in mind. These are the key areas you should always check to evaluate a company's financial reports and ensure you're making informed investment decisions:

- **Healthy Margins (Income Statement)**: Look at the company's profit margins—gross, operating and net margins. Strong and consistent margins show that the company is able to generate profit efficiently from its sales, which is key to long-term growth. Any significant declines in margins should be questioned and investigated further.

- **Manageable Debt-to-Equity Ratio (Balance Sheet):** Check the company's debt levels, particularly the **debt-to-equity ratio**. Too much debt can create financial strain, especially in times of economic downturn or declining sales. A balanced ratio indicates that the company is using debt responsibly to fuel growth without taking on excessive risk.

- **Strong Free Cash Flow (Cash Flow Statement):** Make sure the company is generating enough cash from its operations. Positive free cash flow allows a company to reinvest, pay down debt or return capital to shareholders. Weak or negative free cash flow could be a sign of problems ahead, even if the company is profitable on paper.

- **Spot Potential Red Flags (Manipulation and Inconsistencies):** Finally, keep an eye out for any signs of creative accounting or red flags. These include **inconsistent revenue growth**, sudden **spikes in earnings, unusual changes in liabilities** or **rising Days Sales Outstanding (DSO)**. These could indicate underlying problems, such as manipulation of numbers, poor collections or financial instability.

This checklist provides a quick framework to ensure you're considering all the essential aspects of a company's financial health. By going through these points every time you analyse a company's financial statements, you'll become much more comfortable identifying strong investment opportunities—and avoiding risky ones.

Actionable Next Steps

So, how do you take all this knowledge and put it into action? The first step is to start practising. Take real-world financial statements—whether it's companies you're interested in investing in or even those you're not so sure about—and walk through them using the checklist above. Compare companies within the same industry, evaluate their margins, debt levels and cash flow and see how they stack up against one another. The more you practice, the more you'll start recognising patterns and developing an instinct for spotting strong investments.

If you're looking to apply this to your actual investments, start by picking a company you already own or are considering buying. Pull up its latest **annual report** or **quarterly earnings report** and begin analysing the financial statements using the concepts and tools we've covered. Look for the signs of a healthy company and identify any potential red flags. How does the company's debt-to-equity ratio compare to industry averages? Are margins consistent or are they trending downward? Is there strong free cash flow to support growth?

Don't be discouraged if it takes a while to feel comfortable with this process. Financial statements can be dense and complex, but the more you work through them, the more you'll understand how everything fits together. Over time, you'll start to develop a sharper eye for identifying companies that have solid fundamentals versus those that are overhyped or struggling beneath the surface.

Final Words of Advice: The Importance of Patience and Discipline in Investing

As Warren Buffett always emphasises, **patience and discipline** are essential for successful investing. It's easy to get swept up in short-term market movements, but true wealth is built by investing in companies with strong fundamentals and holding onto them for the long term. Evaluating a company's financial health is not about finding a quick win—it's about identifying businesses that can provide steady, sustainable growth over the years.

Investing is a marathon, not a sprint. The more you understand financial statements and the tools for evaluating a company's health, the better positioned you'll be to make wise, long-term decisions. By combining patience with the knowledge and skills you've gained in this book, you'll be well on your way to becoming a more informed, confident investor—just like Warren Buffett.

Now, go ahead and start practising. Use real financial reports, refine your skills and remember to be patient. Building wealth takes time, but with the right approach, you'll be on the path to success. Happy investing!

www.ingramcontent.com/pod-product-compliance
Lightning Source LLC
Chambersburg PA
CBHW071057240526
45471CB00016B/1978